# THE PILGRIM'S PROGRESS

ILLUSTRATED AND ANNOTATED

## JOHN BUNYAN

*with foreword by* KEN HAM

Petersburg, Kentucky, USA

*The Pilgrim's Progress*
Bunyan, John (1628–1688)
Public Domain

ISBN: 1-893345-90-4
Cover and interior illustrations: Jonathan Taylor
Cover design: Dan Stelzer
Interior layout: Diane King
Project editor: Stacia McKeever
Editors: Rebekah Stelzer, Michael Matthews

Printed in China

# TABLE OF CONTENTS

# FOREWORD

I MUST ADMIT, some people thought my wife Mally and I were a little crazy. Within months after our children were born, we began to read them books and show them the pictures in the books. Although we didn't expect our babies at such a young age to understand what we were reading or showing them, we were applying a biblical principle that we believed was important for the future of our children:

> Train up a child in the way he should go: and when he is old, he will not depart from it (Proverbs 22:6).

This verse is not a guarantee of salvation if parents use a particular formula (after all, each must answer for his or her own sins), but it teaches that training in early years has a great influence on establishing life-long habits.

Based on this verse and many others (e.g., Deuteronomy 6:6–7), we were convinced that the more we taught our children from their earliest years to acquire a taste for the things of the Lord, the more likely they were to retain this taste throughout the rest of their lives.

As toddlers, our children began to like the books we read to them, and eventually they could understand what we were reading. Although they couldn't read, they could see the pictures and follow along. Then they began to read the same books themselves, eventually progressing to other books as they matured and their reading level increased. Yes, we had taught our children to acquire a taste for reading, and in doing so, to acquire a taste for the things of the Lord, because that was the main purpose for which we used these books.

In thinking about this, I'm reminded of the fact that my parents taught me to acquire a taste for a spread called Vegemite. Now, most Americans basically gag if they try to eat Vegemite—but that's understandable. You see, they weren't taught to acquire a taste for Vegemite at a young age as I was. The taste I have for Vegemite was acquired as a child and will be with me for the rest of my life.

That is why I sometimes say that Christian parents need to train up "Vegemite children." In other words, we need to train children from a young age to acquire the right tastes—and the most important taste is for the Word of the Lord and the gospel.

Thinking back to my own childhood, I don't remember most of the books my parents provided for me, except for one book that stands out—*Pilgrim's Progress*. There is something very special about this book—the greatest allegory ever written. It's still in print and a best-seller over 300 years after it was originally published. Most books today last only a few years in print. If a book lasts 10 years it's considered out of the norm.

There is no doubt the Lord has specially blessed *Pilgrim's Progress*. I believe this is because it is a publication for the whole family so all ages can identify with our earthly struggles and understand the blessed message of the gospel.

Even if you've read *Pilgrim's Progress* before, read it again—make it a yearly (or every other year) event. We should never tire of being reminded of the greatest message ever that never changes and is for all ages. As the words of that great hymn state:

> Tell me the old, old story of unseen things above,
> Of Jesus and His glory, of Jesus and His love.
> Tell me the story simply, as to a little child,
> For I am weak and weary, and helpless and defiled.
>
> Tell me the story slowly, that I may take it in,

*That wonderful redemption, God's remedy for sin.*
*Tell me the story often, for I forget so soon;*
*The early dew of morning has passed away at noon.*

*Tell me the same old story when you have cause to fear*
*That this world's empty glory is costing me too dear.*
*Tell me the story always, if you would really be,*
*In any time of trouble a comforter to me.*

*Tell me the old, old story,*
*Tell me the old, old story,*
*Tell me the old, old story of Jesus and His love.*

As you make your pilgrimage through this life, I can't implore you enough to ensure that your family studies God's Word diligently, and also that you use this great classic called *Pilgrim's Progress* as part of your own training and equipping process so your family, friends and others will indeed hear and understand the greatest and most important message ever.

Ken Ham
President, *Answers in Genesis*

# 1

# HISTORICAL BACKGROUND, AUTHOR'S APOLOGY

*PILGRIM'S PROGRESS* (first published in 1678) was written by John Bunyan while he was in a Bedford, England, jail. But why was an itinerant preacher who dearly loved the Word of God writing from a prison cell?

The story of John Bunyan and how he came to be imprisoned actually begins in AD 1324 with the birth of another baby boy named John—John Wycliffe. At that time, Catholicism was the dominant religion in most of Western Europe, including England where Wycliffe lived. Although the Catholic Church has its roots in the New Testament church, gradually over the years, it had accumulated teachings and practices that were contrary to what the Word of God teaches.

John Wycliffe studied theology, law and philosophy at Oxford and eventually became a doctor of theology. He spent a great deal of time studying his Bible. He discovered that what he was learning from Scripture contradicted what the Catholic Church taught, and he set out calling the church back to the authority of God's Word. The "Morning Star of the Reformation," as Wycliffe is called, was responsible for producing the first handwritten version of the Bible in English, enabling thousands of people to know for themselves what God says in His Word. He and his "Bible men" (as their critics called them) preached the *true* gospel of Jesus Christ—that salvation comes through faith by the grace of God (apart from good works as the Church taught) and that the Bible alone (not the Church) was the final authority in all matters of faith and practice.

After Wycliffe's death in 1384, John Hus, one of Wycliffe's disciples, continued the call for church reformation from his home in Prague. Because of his teachings, Hus spent 73 days in confinement, was tried and then condemned to death as a heretic. When asked to recant his beliefs, he said, "In the truth of the gospel which I have written, taught and preached I will die today with gladness." As he was tied to the stake and the fire was kindled beneath him along with the very manuscripts of Wycliffe, Hus cried out, "In 100 years, God will raise up a man whose calls for reform cannot be suppressed!" That was in 1415.

A little over 100 years later, John Hus' words came true in an Augustinian monk named Martin Luther. In 1517, after searching the Scriptures and realizing that salvation came by God's grace alone through faith alone in Jesus Christ alone, Luther posted 95 theses on the church door at Wittenberg, Germany. These statements listed 95 points on which Luther believed that the Church had departed from the teaching of God's Word. When told to recant his statements (which the pope declared "heretical"), Luther said, "Unless I am convinced by proofs from Scriptures or by plain and clear reasons and arguments, I can and will not retract, for it is neither safe nor wise to do anything against conscience. Here I stand. I can do no other. God help me. Amen." He was then forced into exile, during which time he translated the Bible into the common language of the German people. Luther died of natural causes in 1546.

During this time, reformation was continuing in other parts of the world as well. In England, the Roman Catholic Church's blatant disregard for the authority of God's Word can be summed up in this statement by a clergyman to William Tyndale: "We are better to be without God's laws than the Pope's." Outraged, Tyndale replied, "I defy the Pope and all his laws. If God spare my life ere many years, I will cause the boy that drives the plow to know more of the scriptures than you!"

God *did* spare Tyndale's life, which allowed him to translate the New Testament from Greek (Wycliffe had done his translation from the Latin Vulgate) into then-modern English. He used a moveable-type printing press that Johann Gutenberg had invented in the 1450s to print vast quantities of the newly translated Bible, distributing them to the English masses. His work later became the basis for the Authorized King James Version of 1611. Because of his beliefs, Tyndale was imprisoned for 500 days, tried for heresy, convicted and then strangled and burned at the stake in 1536.

It was in 1536 that a young man named John Calvin arrived in Geneva, Switzerland, where the Reformation had already started under the direction of William Farel. Calvin had been forced to flee Paris a few years before after preaching a sermon calling the church to return to the true gospel. He provided organization to the Reformers' thoughts and ideas and wrote the *Institutes of the Christian Religion*.

Although there were differences between what the various Reformers taught, they all united around five main doctrines: *Sola Fide* (by faith alone), *Sola Gratia* (by grace alone), *Sola Scriptura* (by Scripture alone),

*Soli Deo Gloria* (glory to God alone), *Solus Christus* (by Christ alone).

Of course, the radical reform that was sweeping through Europe did not leave governments untouched. Although there was much religious ferment going on everywhere, we'll focus on the events in England leading up to John Bunyan's time.

When Tyndale was martyred, his last words were, "Lord, open the King of England's eyes!" The king on the throne at that time was Henry VIII. He had broken with the Roman Catholic Church (he was upset that the pope would not grant him a divorce from Catherine of Aragon) and declared himself the head of the Church of England. Although he was influenced by the Reformers to some extent and instituted moderate reform in the church, he "remained, in his doctrine, a Roman Catholic to the end of his life."[1]

After Henry died, his son Edward VI (at the age of nine) ascended the throne. Although he was sympathetic to those who desired to reform the church and instituted legislation that supported the Reformers, Edward died when he was sixteen, in 1553.

He was followed by his older sister, Mary I, a staunch Catholic, who overturned the reforming work of her brother. The queen's persecution of the Reformers was merciless and earned her the nickname "Bloody Mary." Although many Protestants were put to death, some fled to the continent, where they came in contact with Reformation leaders such as Calvin, who continued to call for reform in church practices as well as doctrine.

After Mary died, her younger sister Elizabeth I took the throne. "Good Queen Bess," as she was called, en-

---

1    Lloyd-Jones, D. Martyn, *From Puritanism to Nonconformity*, Evangelical Press of Wales, England, p. 12, 1962.

deavored to restore peace to her realm by attempting to build bridges between the various religious ideals. She reasserted England's independence from Rome with the Act of Supremacy in 1559 and attempted to bring order to the Church of England with the Act of Uniformity, also in 1559. This act required that every man assent to the *Book of Common Prayers* and attend church once a week or be fined. However, the prayer book contained teaching which the Puritans (a group which desired to reform the church completely from within) rejected as unbiblical. This led those who disagreed to leave the Anglican church (although a few Puritans decided to stay and continue to push for reform within the church). Those who followed a man named Robert Browne became known as Brownists or Separatists, while those who followed Thomas Cartwright were known as Presbyterians. Persecution of those not part of the established church increased throughout Elizabeth's reign.

After the death of Elizabeth in 1603, her cousin James I (then king of Scotland) ruled England and Scotland jointly for the next 22 years. The Puritans thought that James would be sympathetic to their ideas because he came from the Presbyterian Church of Scotland. However, James was more concerned with power than truth; and although he convened a conference to discuss the Puritans' petitions, those attending the conference were leaders of the Anglican church who had strayed even further from biblical teaching and opposed Puritan thought. You may have heard of the main product of this conference: the 1611 King James Bible (over 70% of which was based on Tyndale's translation).

Because life was becoming more unbearable for them, many left the country. In fact, it was in 1620 that the voyage of the *Mayflower* took place, bringing the Pilgrims to American soil. The Plymouth Colony was settled by the Pilgrims (or Separatists) in 1620. The Massachusetts Bay Colony (1628) was settled by the Puritans (or, as they called themselves, "Non-separating Congregationalists" since they did not consider themselves to have separated from the Church of England, although they separated themselves from its errors).

In 1625 James died and his son Charles I became king. Three years later, John Bunyan, the author of our story about Pilgrim, was born into this religious and political turmoil, which would only get worse.

King Charles and Archbishop Laud worked to enforce Elizabeth's Act of Uniformity in various ways, forcing everyone to conform to the teachings of the church. Those of a "tender conscience" were grieved by these teachings and practices and refused to conform, facing severe persecution. Eventually, Charles I and the archbishop attempted to make the Scots also conform. But instead, the Scots rebelled and introduced the National Covenant.

The religious and political turmoil caused a divide between Parliament and the king and resulted in a war between those loyal to the king (known as "Royalists" or "Cavaliers") and those (called "Roundheads") who agreed with the changes Parliament wanted to make in the government and the Church of England. Oliver Cromwell, a vibrant Puritan, became the commander of the parliamentary army (of which Bunyan was a member from 1644–1647) and eventually led them to victory over the Cavaliers. Charles I was tried for treason in 1648 and executed in 1649.

Cromwell abolished the monarchy, and England became a commonwealth with Cromwell as the Lord Protector of the Realm. The Puritans experienced great religious freedom and tolerance during his leadership (1649–1658).

During this time John Bunyan married and began an intense spiritual struggle (lasting from 1648 to 1652), which is chronicled in *Grace Abounding to the Chief of Sinners* and reflected in *Pilgrim's Progress* in various places. At some point in his ordeal, Bunyan encountered Martin Luther's commentary on Galatians, which encouraged him greatly that he was not alone in the struggles and temptations he was facing. Of Luther's commentary, Bunyan later wrote in *Grace Abounding*:

> It also was so old that it was ready to fall piece from piece if I did but turn it over. Now I was pleased much that such an old book had fallen into my hands; the which, when I had but a little way perused, I found my condition, in his experience, so largely and profoundly handled, as if his book had been written out of my heart. This made me marvel; for thus thought I, This man could not know anything of the state of Christians now, but must needs write and speak the experience of former days. … I do prefer this book of Martin Luther upon the Galatians, excepting the Holy Bible, before all the books that ever I have seen, as most fit for a wounded conscience.

John Gifford (after whom Evangelist, in *Pilgrim's*

*Progress*, is modeled) also served as a spiritual mentor to Bunyan. In 1653, after finally being assured that he was indeed a child of God who had been chosen from before the foundation of the world and whose sins had been forgiven, Bunyan joined Gifford's independent congregation (which was not part of the state church) in Bedford, England. He also began preaching at various places around the countryside, drawing on his own experiences and knowledge of the Scriptures since he had no formal training.

He continued preaching until Cromwell died and the monarchy, under Charles II, was restored in April 1660. The king began at once to withdraw the religious freedom the country had experienced, and those who refused to conform to the king's decrees were incarcerated under the Elizabethan Act of Uniformity (see above). The "Nonconformists" refused to use the *Book of Common Prayer* or to attend services at "state" churches, and instead used the Bible to guide them and attended local gatherings of like-minded believers.

In November 1660, Bunyan was arrested for not conforming to the king's edicts and spent the next twelve years in jail. When he was questioned by a Mr. Cobb about whether or not he would "leave off" preaching, Bunyan responded by quoting the Morning Star of the Reformation, "Wyckliffe saith that he which leaveth off preaching and learning of the Word of God for fear of excommunication of men, he is already excommunicated of God, and shall in the day of judgment be counted a traitor to Christ."[2]

During his imprisonment, he supported his family by making shoe laces and writing several

---

2   A Relation of the Imprisonment of Mr. John Bunyan, Minister of the Gospel at Bedford in November, 1660, by John Bunyan, MDCCLXV. Bunyan probably knew of Wycliffe through reading John Foxe's Book of Martyrs, which was one of the only two books Bunyan had with him while in jail—the other was the Bible.

books (among them *Profitable Meditations*, *Christian Behaviour*, *The Holy City* and *Grace Abounding to the Chief of Sinners*). He was released from jail because of a royal pardon in May 1672 and became pastor of the independent church at Bedford, which was meeting in a barn.

All of this finally brings us to 1677 when John Bunyan was once again jailed for preaching without license. He spent six months in a jail on a bridge over the River Ouse. It was here that Bunyan finished penning his most famous work, *Pilgrim's Progress*, which he originally wrote to entertain his children when they came to the one-room jail to visit him.

After being released from prison, John Bunyan spent his remaining years writing and preaching around the countryside. He died on September 3, 1688, from a cold he caught after being drenched in a heavy downpour while trying to reconcile a father and son. His tomb (pictured here) is in Bunhill Fields, outside of London, where he is buried with other Nonconformists.

# AUTHOR'S APOLOGY[3]

WHEN AT the first I took my pen in hand
Thus for to write, I did not understand
That I at all should make a little book
In such a mode: nay, I had undertook
To make another; which, when almost done,
Before I was aware I this begun.

And thus it was: I, writing of the way
And race of saints in this our gospel-day,
Fell suddenly into an allegory
About their journey, and the way to glory,
In more than twenty things which I set down
This done, I twenty more had in my crown,
And they again began to multiply,
Like sparks that from the coals of fire do fly.
Nay, then, thought I, if that you breed so fast,
I'll put you by yourselves, lest you at last
Should prove *ad infinitum*, and eat out
The book that I already am about.
Well, so I did; but yet I did not think
To show to all the world my pen and ink
In such a mode; I only thought to make
I knew not what: nor did I undertake
Thereby to please my neighbor; no, not I;
I did it my own self to gratify.

Neither did I but vacant seasons spend
In this my scribble; nor did I intend
But to divert myself, in doing this,
From worser thoughts, which make me do amiss.
Thus I set pen to paper with delight,

---

3  *This section was written by John Bunyan to explain to his readership why he wrote it and to counter many of the criticisms he received about it.*

And quickly had my thoughts in black and white;
For having now my method by the end,
Still as I pull'd, it came; and so I penned
It down; until it came at last to be,
For length and breadth, the bigness which you see.

    Well, when I had thus put mine ends together
I show'd them others, that I might see whether
They would condemn them, or them justify:
And some said, let them live; some, let them die:
Some said, John, print it; others said, Not so:
Some said, It might do good; others said, No.

    Now was I in a strait, and did not see
Which was the best thing to be done by me:
At last I thought, Since ye are thus divided,
I print it will; and so the case decided.

    For, thought I, some I see would have it done,
Though others in that channel do not run:
To prove, then, who advised for the best,
Thus I thought fit to put it to the test.

    I further thought, if now I did deny
Those that would have it, thus to gratify;
I did not know, but hinder them I might
Of that which would to them be great delight.
For those which were not for its coming forth,
I said to them, Offend you, I am loath;
Yet since your brethren pleased with it be,
Forbear to judge, till you do further see.

    If that thou wilt not read, let it alone;
Some love the meat, some love to pick the bone.
Yea, that I might them better palliate,
I did too with them thus expostulate:

    May I not write in such a style as this?
In such a method too, and yet not miss
My end—thy good? Why may it not be done?
Dark clouds bring waters, when the bright bring none.
Yea, dark or bright, if they their silver drops
Cause to descend, the earth, by yielding crops,

Gives praise to both, and carpeth not at either,
But treasures up the fruit they yield together;
Yea, so commixes both, that in their fruit
None can distinguish this from that; they suit
Her well when hungry; but if she be full,
She spews out both, and makes their blessing null.
　　You see the ways the fisherman doth take
To catch the fish; what engines doth he make!
Behold how he engageth all his wits;
Also his snares, lines, angles, hooks, and nets:
　　Yet fish there be, that neither hook nor line,
Nor snare, nor net, nor engine can make thine:
They must be groped for, and be tickled too,
Or they will not be catch'd, whate'er you do.
　　How does the fowler seek to catch his game
By divers means! all which one cannot name.
His guns, his nets, his lime-twigs, light and bell:
He creeps, he goes, he stands; yea, who can tell
Of all his postures? yet there's none of these
Will make him master of what fowls he please.
Yea, he must pipe and whistle, to catch *this*;
Yet if he does so, *that* bird he will miss.
If that a pearl may in toad's head dwell,
And may be found too in an oyster-shell;
If things that promise nothing, do contain
What better is than gold; who will disdain,
That have an inkling of it, there to look,
That they may find it. Now my little book,
(Though void of all these paintings that may make
It with this or the other man to take,)
Is not without those things that do excel
What do in brave but empty notions dwell.
　　"Well, yet I am not fully satisfied
That this your book will stand, when soundly tried."
　　Why, what's the matter? "It is dark." What though?
"But it is feigned." What of that? I trow
Some men by feigned words, as dark as mine,

Make truth to spangle, and its rays to shine.
"But they want solidness." Speak, man, thy mind.
"They drown the weak; metaphors make us blind."
    Solidity, indeed, becomes the pen
Of him that writeth things divine to men:
But must I needs want solidness, because
By metaphors I speak? Were not God's laws,
His gospel laws, in olden time held forth
By types, shadows, and metaphors? Yet loth
Will any sober man be to find fault
With them, lest he be found for to assault
The highest wisdom! No, he rather stoops,
And seeks to find out what, by pins and loops,
By calves and sheep, by heifers, and by rams,
By birds and herbs, and by the blood of lambs,
God speaketh to him; and happy is he
That finds the light and grace that in them be.
    But not too forward, therefore, to conclude
That I want solidness—that I am rude;
All things solid in show, not solid be;
All things in parable despise not we,
Lest things most hurtful lightly we receive,
And things that good are, of our souls bereave.
My dark and cloudy words they do but hold
The truth, as cabinets inclose the gold.
    The prophets used much by metaphors
To set forth truth: yea, who so considers
Christ, his apostles too, shall plainly see,
That truths to this day in such mantles be.
    Am I afraid to say, that holy writ,
Which for its style and phrase puts down all wit,
Is everywhere so full of all these things,
Dark figures, allegories? Yet there springs
From that same book, that lustre, and those rays
Of light, that turn our darkest nights to days.
    Come, let my carper to his life now look,
And find there darker lines than in my book

He findeth any; yea, and let him know,
That in his best things there are worse lines too.
    May we but stand before impartial men,
To his poor one I durst adventure ten,
That they will take my meaning in these lines
Far better than his lies in silver shrines.
Come, truth, although in swaddling-clothes, I find
Informs the judgment, rectifies the mind;
Pleases the understanding, makes the will
Submit, the memory too it doth fill
With what doth our imagination please;
Likewise it tends our troubles to appease.
    Sound words, I know, Timothy is to use,
And old wives' fables he is to refuse;
But yet grave Paul him nowhere doth forbid
The use of parables, in which lay hid
That gold, those pearls, and precious stones that were
Worth digging for, and that with greatest care.
    Let me add one word more. O man of God,
Art thou offended? Dost thou wish I had
Put forth my matter in another dress?
Or that I had in things been more express?
Three things let me propound; then I submit
To those that are my betters, as is fit.
    1. I find not that I am denied the use
Of this my method, so I no abuse
Put on the words, things, readers, or be rude
In handling figure or similitude,
In application; but all that I may
Seek the advance of truth this or that way.
Denied, did I say? Nay, I have leave,
(Example too, and that from them that have
God better pleased, by their words or ways,
Than any man that breatheth now-a-days,)
Thus to express my mind, thus to declare
Things unto thee that excellentest are.
    2. I find that men as high as trees will write

Dialogue-wise; yet no man doth them slight
For writing so. Indeed, if they abuse
Truth, cursed be they, and the craft they use
To that intent; but yet let truth be free
To make her sallies upon thee and me,
Which way it pleases God: for who knows how,
Better than he that taught us first to plough,
To guide our minds and pens for his designs?
And he makes base things usher in divine.

    3. I find that holy writ, in many places,
Hath semblance with this method, where the cases
Do call for one thing to set forth another:
Use it I may then, and yet nothing smother
Truth's golden beams: nay, by this method may
Make it cast forth its rays as light as day.

    And now, before I do put up my pen,
I'll show the profit of my book; and then
Commit both thee and it unto that hand
That pulls the strong down, and makes weak ones stand.

    This book it chalketh out before thine eyes
The man that seeks the everlasting prize:
It shows you whence he comes, whither he goes,
What he leaves undone; also what he does:
It also shows you how he runs, and runs,
Till he unto the gate of glory comes.
It shows, too, who set out for life amain,
As if the lasting crown they would obtain;
Here also you may see the reason why
They lose their labor, and like fools do die.

    This book will make a traveler of thee,
If by its counsel thou wilt ruled be;
It will direct thee to the Holy Land,
If thou wilt its directions understand
Yea, it will make the slothful active be;
The blind also delightful things to see.

    Art thou for something rare and profitable?
Or would'st thou see a truth within a fable?

Art thou forgetful? Wouldest thou remember
From New-Year's day to the last of December?
Then read my fancies; they will stick like burs,
And may be, to the helpless, comforters.

    This book is writ in such a dialect
As may the minds of listless men affect:
It seems a novelty, and yet contains
Nothing but sound and honest gospel strains.

    Would'st thou divert thyself from melancholy?
Would'st thou be pleasant, yet be far from folly?
Would'st thou read riddles, and their explanation?
Or else be drowned in thy contemplation?
Dost thou love picking meat? Or would'st thou see
A man i' the clouds, and hear him speak to thee?
Would'st thou be in a dream, and yet not sleep?
Or would'st thou in a moment laugh and weep?
Would'st thou lose thyself and catch no harm,
And find thyself again without a charm?
Would'st read thyself, and read thou know'st not what,
And yet know whether thou art blest or not,
By reading the same lines? O then come hither,
And lay my book, thy head, and heart together.

# 2

# CHRISTIAN

# &

# EVANGELIST

A S I walked through the wilderness of this world, I lighted on a certain place where was a den,[1] and laid me down in that place to sleep; and as I slept, I dreamed a dream. I dreamed, and behold, I saw a man clothed with rags, standing in a certain place, with his face from his own house, a book in his hand, and a great burden upon his back. I looked and saw him open the book, and read therein; and as he read, he wept and trembled; and not being able longer to contain, he brake out with a lamentable cry, saying, "What shall I do?"

*Isaiah 64:6*
*Luke 14:33*
*Psalm 38:4*

*Acts 2:37; 16:30*
*Habakkuk 1:2–3*

In this plight, therefore, he went home, and re-strained himself as long as he could, that his wife and children should not perceive his distress; but he could not be silent long, because that his trouble increased. Wherefore at length he brake his mind to his wife and children; and thus he began to talk to them: "O, my dear wife," said he, "and you the children of my bowels, I, your dear friend, am in myself undone by reason of a burden that lieth hard upon me; moreover, I am certainly

---

1  *Bedford jail, in which the author was imprisoned for conscience' sake*

informed that this our city will be burnt with fire from heaven; in which fearful overthrow, both myself, with thee my wife, and you my sweet babes, shall miserably come to ruin, except (the which yet I see not) some way of escape can be found whereby we may be delivered."

At this his relations were sore amazed; not for that they believed that what he had said to them was true, but because they thought that some frenzy distemper had got into his head; therefore, it draw-

ing towards night, and they hoping that sleep might settle his brains, with all haste they got him to bed. But the night was as troublesome to him as the day; wherefore, instead of sleeping, he spent it in sighs and tears. So when the morning was come, they would know how he did. He told them, "Worse and worse:" he also set to talking to them again; but they began to be hardened. They also thought to drive away his distemper by harsh and surly carriage to him; sometimes they would deride, sometimes they would chide, and sometimes they would quite neglect him. Wherefore he began to retire himself to his chamber to pray for and pity them, and also to condole his own misery; he would also walk solitarily in the fields, sometimes reading, and sometimes praying: and thus for some days he spent his time.

Now I saw, upon a time, when he was walking in the fields, that he was (as he was wont) reading in his book, and greatly distressed in his mind; and as he read, he burst out, as he had done before, crying, "What shall I do to be saved?"

*Acts 16:30–31*

I saw also that he looked this way, and that way, as if he would run; yet he stood still because (as I perceived) he could not tell which way to go. I looked then, and saw a man named Evangelist coming to him, and he asked, "Wherefore dost thou cry?"

*Hebrews 9:27*
*Job 10:21–22*
*Ezekiel 22:14*

He answered, "Sir, I perceive, by the book in my hand, that I am condemned to die, and after that to come to judgment, and I find that I am not willing to do the first, nor able to do the second."

Then said Evangelist, "Why not willing to die, since this life is attended with so many evils?" The man answered, "Because, I fear that this burden that is upon my back will sink me lower than the grave, and I shall fall into Tophet. And Sir, if I be not fit to go to prison, I am not fit to go to judgment, and from thence to execution; and the thoughts of these things make me cry."

*Isaiah 30:33*

Then said Evangelist, "If this be thy condition, why standest thou still?" He answered, "Because I know not whither to go." Then he gave him a parchment roll, and there was written within, "Fly from the wrath to come."

*Matthew 3:7*

*Matthew 7:13–14*

The man therefore read it, and looking upon Evangelist very carefully, said, "Whither must I fly?" Then said Evangelist, (pointing with his finger over a very wide field,) "Do you see yonder wicket-gate?" The

man said, "No." Then said the other, "Do you see yonder shining light?" He said, "I think I do." Then said Evangelist, "Keep that light in your eye, and go up directly thereto, so shalt thou see the gate; at which, when thou knockest, it shall be told thee what thou shalt do."

*Psalm 119:105*
*2 Peter 1:19*

# 3

# Obstinate

# &

# Pliable

So I saw in my dream that the man began to run. Now he had not run far from his own door when his wife and children, perceiving it, began to cry after him to return; but the man put his fingers in his ears, and ran on crying, Life! life! eternal life! So he looked not behind him, but fled towards the middle of the plain.

*Luke 14:26*
*Genesis 19:17*
*Jeremiah 20:10*

The neighbors also came out to see him run; and as he ran, some mocked, others threatened, and some cried after him to return; and among those that did so, there were two that were resolved to fetch him back by force. The name of the one was Obstinate and the name of the other Pliable. Now by this time the man was got a good distance from them; but, however, they were resolved to pursue him, which they did, and in a little time they overtook him. Then said the man, "Neighbors, wherefore are you come?" They said, "To persuade you to go back with us." But he said, "That can by no means be: you dwell," said he, "in the city of Destruction, the place also where I was born: I see it to be so; and dying there, sooner or later, you will sink lower than the grave, into a place that burns with fire and brimstone: be content, good neighbors, and go along with me."

OBSTINATE: What, said Obstinate, and leave our friends and our comforts behind us!

CHRISTIAN: Yes, said Christian, (for that was his name,) because that all which you forsake is not worthy to be compared with a little of that I am seeking to enjoy; and if you will go along with me, and hold it, you shall fare as I myself; for there, where I go, is enough and to spare. Come away, and prove my words.

*2 Corinthians 4:18*

*Luke 15:17*

OBSTINATE: What are the things you seek, since you leave all the world to find them?

CHRISTIAN: I seek an inheritance incorrupt-ible, undefiled, and that fadeth not away; and it is laid up in heaven, and safe there to be bestowed, at the time appointed, on them<sup>Hebrews 11:16</sup> that diligently seek it. Read it so, if you will, in my book.

*1 Peter 1:4*

OBSTINATE: Tush, said Obstinate, away with your book; will you go back with us or no?

CHRISTIAN: No, not I, said the other, because I have laid my hand to the plough.

*Luke 9:62*

OBSTINATE: Come then, neighbor Pliable, let us turn again, and go home without him: there is a company of these crazy-headed coxcombs, that when they take a fancy by the end, are wis-er in their own eyes than seven men that can render a reason.

PLIABLE: Then said Pliable, Don't revile; if what the good Christian says is true, the things he looks after are better than ours: my heart in-clines to go with my neighbor.

OBSTINATE: What, more fools still! Be ruled by me, and go back; who knows whither such a brain-sick fellow will lead you? Go back, go back, and be wise.

CHRISTIAN: Nay, but do thou come with thy neighbor Pliable; there are such things to be had which I spoke of, and many more glories besides. If you believe not me, read here in this book, and for the truth of what is expressed therein, behold, all is confirmed by the blood of Him

*Hebrews 9:17–21*

that made it.

PLIABLE: Well, neighbor Obstinate, said Pliable, I begin to come to a point; I intend to go along with this good man, and to cast in my lot with him: but, my good companion, do you know the way to this desired place?

CHRISTIAN: I am directed by a man whose name is Evangelist, to speed me to a little gate that is before us, where we shall receive instructions about the way.

PLIABLE: Come then, good neighbor, let us be going. Then they went both together.

OBSTINATE: And I will go back to my place, said Obstinate: I will be no companion of such misled, fantastical fellows.

Now I saw in my dream, that when Obstinate was gone back, Christian and Pliable went talking over the plain; and thus they began their discourse.

CHRISTIAN: Come, neighbor Pliable, how do you do? I am glad you are persuaded to go along with me. Had even Obstinate himself but felt what I have felt of the powers and terrors of what is yet unseen, he would not thus lightly have given us the back.

PLIABLE: Come, neighbor Christian, since there are none but us two here, tell me now farther, what the things are, and how to be enjoyed, whither we are going.

CHRISTIAN: I can better conceive of them with my mind, than speak of them with my tongue: but yet, since you are desirous to know, I will read of them in my book.

PLIABLE: And do you think that the words of your book are certainly true?

CHRISTIAN: Yes, verily; for it was made by Him that cannot lie.

PLIABLE: Well said; what things are they?

CHRISTIAN: There is an endless kingdom to be inhabited, and everlasting life to be given us, that we may inhabit that kingdom for ever.

*Isaiah 65:17*
*John 10:27–29*

PLIABLE: Well said; and what else?

CHRISTIAN: There are crowns of glory to be given us; and garments that will make us shine like the sun in the firmament of heaven.

*2 Timothy 4:8*
*Revelation 22:5*
*Matthew 13:43*

PLIABLE: This is very pleasant; and what else?

CHRISTIAN: There shall be no more crying, nor sorrow; for he that is owner of the place will wipe all tears from our eyes.

*Isaiah 25:8*
*Revelation 7:16–17; 21:4*

# 4

# SLOUGH OF
# DESPOND & HELP

PLIABLE: AND what company shall we have there?

CHRISTIAN: There we shall be with seraphims and cherubims, creatures that will dazzle your eyes to look on them. There also you shall meet with thousands and ten thousands that have gone before us to that place; none of them are hurtful, but loving and holy; every one walking in the sight of God, and standing in his presence with acceptance for ever. In a word, there we shall see the elders with their golden crowns; there we shall see the holy virgins with their golden harps; there we shall see men, that by the world were cut in pieces, burnt in flames, eaten of beasts, drowned in the seas, for the love they bare to the Lord of the place, all well, and clothed with immortality as with a garment.

*Isaiah 6:2*
*1 Thessalonians 4:16–17*
*Revelation 5:11*

*Revelation 4:4*
*Revelation 14:1–5*

*John 12:25*

*2 Corinthians 5:2*

PLIABLE: The hearing of this is enough to ravish one's heart. But are these things to be enjoyed? How shall we get to be sharers thereof?

CHRISTIAN: The Lord, the governor of the

Isaiah 55:1, 2
John 6:37; 7:37
Revelation 21:6;
22:17

country, hath recorded that in this book, the substance of which is, if we be truly willing to have it, he will bestow it upon us freely.

PLIABLE: Well, my good companion, glad am I to hear of these things: come on, let us mend our pace.

CHRISTIAN: I cannot go as fast as I would, by reason of this burden that is on my back.

Now I saw in my dream, that just as they had ended this talk, they drew nigh to a very miry slough that was in the midst of the plain: and they being heedless, did both fall suddenly into the bog. The name of the slough was Despond. Here, therefore, they wallowed for a time, being grievously bedaubed with the dirt; and Christian, because of the burden that was on his back, began to sink in the mire.

PLIABLE: Then said Pliable, Ah, neighbor Christian, where are you now?

CHRISTIAN: Truly, said Christian, I do not know.

PLIABLE: At this Pliable began to be offended, and angrily said to his fellow, Is this the happiness you have told me all this while of? If we have such ill speed at our first setting out, what may we expect between this and our journey's end? May I get out again with my life, you shall possess the brave country alone for me.

And with that he gave a desperate struggle or two, and got out of the mire on that side of the slough which was next to his own house: so away he went, and Christian saw him no more.

Wherefore Christian was left to tumble in the Slough of Despond alone; but still he endeavored to struggle to that side of the slough that was farthest from his own house, and next to the wicket-gate; the which he did, but could not get out because of the burden that was upon his back: but I beheld in my dream, that a man came to him, whose name was Help, and asked him what he did there.

CHRISTIAN: Sir, said Christian, I was bid to go this way by a man called Evangelist, who directed me also to yonder gate, that I might escape the wrath to come. And as I was going thither, I fell in here.

HELP: But why did not you look for the steps?

CHRISTIAN: Fear followed me so hard that I fled the next way, and fell in.

HELP: Then, said he, Give me thine hand.

*Psalm 40:2*

So he gave him his hand, and he drew him out, and he set him upon sound ground, and bid him go on his way.

Then I stepped to him that plucked him out, and said, "Sir, wherefore, since over this place is the way from the city of Destruction to yonder gate, is it, that this plat is not mended, that poor travellers might go thither with more security?" And he said unto me, "This miry slough is such a place as cannot be mended: it is the descent whither the scum and filth that attends conviction for sin doth continually run, and therefore it is called the Slough of Despond; for still, as the sinner is awakened about his lost condition, there arise in his soul many fears and doubts, and discouraging apprehensions, which all of them get together, and settle in this place: and this is the reason of the badness of this ground.

*Isaiah 35:3–4*

"It is not the pleasure of the King that this place should remain so bad. His laborers also have, by the direction of his Majesty's surveyors, been for above this sixteen hundred years employed about this patch of ground, if perhaps it might have been mended: yea, and to my knowledge," said he, "there have been swallowed up at least twenty thousand cart loads, yea, millions of wholesome instructions, that have at all seasons been brought from all places of the King's dominions, (and they that can tell, say, they are the best materials to make good ground of the place,) if so be it might have been mended; but it is the Slough of Despond still, and so will be when they have done what they can.

"True, there are, by the direction of the Lawgiver, certain good and substantial steps, placed even through the very midst of this slough; but at such time as this place doth much spew out its filth, as it doth against change of weather, these steps are hardly seen; or if they be, men, through the dizziness of their heads, step beside, and then they are bemired to purpose, notwithstanding the steps be there: but the ground is good when they are once got in at the gate."

*1 Samuel 12:23*

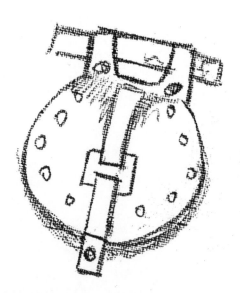

# 5

# MR. WORLDLY
# WISEMAN

N OW I saw in my dream, that by this time Pliable
was got home to his house. So his neighbors came
to visit him; and some of them called him wise man
for coming back, and some called him fool for hazarding himself with Christian: others again did mock at his
cowardliness, saying, "Surely, since you began to venture, I would not have been so base as to have given
out for a few difficulties:" so Pliable sat sneaking among
them. But at last he got more confidence, and then they
all turned their tales, and began to deride poor Christian
behind his back. And thus much concerning Pliable.

Now as Christian was walking solitary by himself, he
espied one afar off come crossing over the field to meet
him; and their hap was to meet just as they were crossing the way of each other. The gentleman's name that
met him was Mr. Wordly Wiseman: he dwelt in the
town of Carnal Policy, a very great town, and also hard
by from whence Christian came. This man then, meeting with Christian, and having some inkling of him,
(for Christian's setting forth from the city of Destruction
was much noised abroad, not only in the town where he
dwelt, but also it began to be the town-talk in some other
places)—Mr. Worldly Wiseman, therefore, having some
guess of him, by beholding his laborious going, by observing his sighs and groans, and the like, began thus to enter

into some talk with Christian.

MR. WORLDLY WISEMAN: How now, good fellow, whither away after this burdened manner?

CHRISTIAN: A burdened manner indeed, as ever I think poor creature had! And whereas you ask me, Whither away? I tell you, sir, I am going to yonder wicket-gate before me; for there, as I am informed, I shall be put into a way to be rid of my heavy burden.

MR. WORLDLY WISEMAN: Hast thou a wife and children?

CHRISTIAN: Yes; but I am so laden with this burden, that I cannot take that pleasure in them as formerly: methinks I am as if I had none.

*1 Corinthians 7:29*

MR. WORLDLY WISEMAN: Wilt thou hearken to me, if I give thee counsel?

CHRISTIAN: If it be good, I will; for I stand in need of good counsel.

MR. WORLDLY WISEMAN: I would advise thee, then, that thou with all speed get thyself rid of thy burden; for thou wilt never be settled in thy mind till then: nor canst thou enjoy the benefits of the blessings which God hath bestowed upon thee till then.

CHRISTIAN: That is that which I seek for, even to be rid of this heavy burden: but get it off myself I cannot, nor is there any man in our country that can take it off my shoulders; therefore am I going this way, as I told you, that I may be rid of my burden.

MR. WORLDLY WISEMAN: Who bid thee go this way to be rid of thy burden?

CHRISTIAN: A man that appeared to me to be a very great and honorable person: his name, as I remember, is Evangelist.

MR. WORDLY WISEMAN: I beshrew him for his counsel! there is not a more dangerous and troublesome way in the world than is that into which he hath directed thee; and that thou shalt find, if thou wilt be ruled by his counsel. Thou hast met with something, as I perceive, already; for I see the dirt of the Slough of Despond is upon thee: but that slough is the beginning of the sorrows that do attend those that go on in that way. Hear me; I am older than thou: thou art like to meet with, in the way which thou goest, wearisomeness, painfulness, hunger, perils, nakedness, sword, lions, dragons, darkness, and, in a word, death, and what not. These things are certainly true, having been confirmed by many testimonies. And should a man so carelessly cast away himself, by giving heed to a stranger?

CHRISTIAN: Why, sir, this burden on my back is more terrible to me than are all these things which you have mentioned: nay, methinks I care not what I meet with in the way, if so be I can also meet with deliverance from my burden.

MR. WORLDLY WISEMAN: How camest thou by thy burden at first?

CHRISTIAN: By reading this book in my hand.

MR. WORLDLY WISEMAN: I thought so; and it has happened unto thee as to other weak men, who, meddling with things too high for them, do suddenly fall into thy distractions; which distractions do not only unman men, as thine I perceive have done thee, but they run them upon desperate ventures, to obtain they know not what.

CHRISTIAN: I know what I would obtain; it is ease from my heavy burden.

MR. WORLDLY WISEMAN: But why wilt thou seek for ease this way, seeing so many dangers attend it? especially since (hadst thou but patience to hear me) I could direct thee to the obtaining of what thou desirest, without the dangers that thou in this way wilt run thyself into. Yea, and the remedy is at hand. Besides, I will add, that instead of those dangers, thou shalt meet with much safety, friendship, and content.

CHRISTIAN: Sir, I pray open this secret to me.

MR. WORLDLY WISEMAN: Why, in yonder village (the village is named Morality) there dwells a gentleman whose name is Legality, a very judicious man, and a man of a very good name, that has skill to help men off with such burdens as thine is from their shoulders; yea to my knowledge, he hath done a great deal of good this way; aye, and besides, he hath skill to cure those that are somewhat crazed in their wits with their burdens. To him, as I said, thou mayest go, and be helped presently. His house is not quite a mile from this place; and if he should not be at home himself, he hath a pretty young man to his son, whose name is Civility, that can do it (to speak on) as well as the old gentleman himself: there, I say, thou mayest be eased of thy burden; and if thou art not minded to go back to thy former habitation, (as indeed I would not wish thee,) thou mayest send for thy wife and children to this village, where there are houses now standing empty, one of which thou may- est have at a reasonable rate: provision is there also cheap and good; and that which will make thy life the more happy is, to be sure there thou shalt live by honest neighbors, in credit and good fashion.

# 6

# SINAI & EVANGELIST

NOW WAS Christian somewhat at a stand; but presently he concluded, If this be true which this gentleman hath said, my wisest course is to take his advice: and with that he thus farther spake.

> CHRISTIAN: Sir, which is my way to this honest man's house?

> MR. WORLDLY WISEMAN: Do you see yonder high hill?

> CHRISTIAN: Yes, very well.

> MR. WORLDLY WISEMAN: By that hill you must go, and the first house you come at is his.

So Christian turned out of his way to go to Mr. Legality's house for help: but, behold, when he was got now hard by the hill, it seemed so high, and also that side of it that was next the way-side did hang so much over, that Christian was afraid to venture further, lest the hill should fall on his head; wherefore there he stood still, and wotted not what to do. Also his burden now seemed heavier to him than while he was in his way. There came also flashes of fire out of the hill, that made Christian afraid that he should be burnt: here therefore he did sweat and quake for fear.

*Exodus 19:16, 18*

*Hebrews 12:21*

> When Christians until carnal men give ear,
> Out of their way they go, and pay for dear

For Master Worldly Wiseman can but show
A saint the way to bondage and to woe.

And now he began to be sorry that he had taken
Mr. Worldly Wiseman's counsel; and with that he saw
Evangelist coming to meet him, at the sight also of whom
he began to blush for shame. So Evangelist drew nearer
and nearer; and coming up to him, he looked upon him,
with a severe and dreadful countenance, and thus began
to reason with Christian.

EVANGELIST: What doest thou here, Christian? said he: at which words Christian knew not what to answer; wherefore at present he stood speechless before him. Then said Evangelist farther, Art not thou the man that I found crying without the walls of the city of Destruction?

CHRISTIAN: Yes, dear sir, I am the man.

EVANGELIST: Did not I direct thee the way to the little wicket-gate?

CHRISTIAN: Yes, dear sir, said Christian.

EVANGELIST: How is it then thou art so quickly turned aside? For thou art now out of the way.

CHRISTIAN: I met with a gentleman so soon as I had got over the Slough of Despond, who persuaded me that I might, in the village before me, find a man that could take off my burden.

EVANGELIST: What was he?

CHRISTIAN: He looked like a gentleman, and talked much to me, and got me at last to yield: so I came hither; but when I beheld this hill, and how it hangs over the way, I suddenly made a stand, lest it should fall on my head.

EVANGELIST: What said that gentleman to you?

CHRISTIAN: Why, he asked me whither I was going; and I told him.

EVANGELIST: And what said he then?

CHRISTIAN: He asked me if I had a family; and I told him. But, said I, I am so laden with the burden that is on my back, that I cannot take pleasure in them as formerly.

EVANGELIST: And what said he then?

CHRISTIAN: He bid me with speed get rid of my burden; and I told him it was ease that I sought. And, said I, I am therefore going to yonder gate, to receive farther direction how I may get to the place of deliverance. So he said that he would show me a better way, and short, not so attended with difficulties as the way, sir, that you set me in; which way, said he, will direct you to a gentleman's house that hath skill to take off these burdens: so I believed him, and turned out of that way into this, if haply I might be soon eased of my burden. But when I came to this place, and beheld things as they are, I stopped, for fear (as I said) of danger: but I now know not what to do.

EVANGELIST: Then said Evangelist, Stand still a little, that I show thee the words of God. So he stood trembling. Then said Evangelist, "See that ye refuse not Him that speaketh; for if they escaped not who refused him that spake on earth, much more shall not we escape, if we turn away from Him that speaketh from heaven." He said, moreover, "Now the just shall live by faith; but if any man draw back, my soul shall have no pleasure in him." He also did thus apply them: Thou art the man that art running into this misery; thou hast begun to reject the counsel of the Most High, and to draw back thy foot from the way of peace, even almost to the hazarding of thy perdition.

*Hebrews 12:25*

*Hebrews 10:38*

Then Christian fell down at his feet as dead, crying,

Woe is me, for I am undone! At the sight of which Evangelist caught him by the right hand, saying, "All manner of sin and blasphemies shall be forgiven unto men." "Be not faithless, but believing." Then did Christian again a little revive, and stood up trembling, as at first, before Evangelist.

*Matthew 12:31*
*John 20:27*

Then Evangelist proceeded, saying, Give more earnest heed to the things that I shall tell thee of. I will now show thee who it was that deluded thee, and who it was also to whom he sent thee. The man that met thee is one Worldly Wiseman, and rightly is he so called; partly because he savoreth only the doctrine of this world (therefore he always goes to the town of Morality to church;) and partly because he loveth that doctrine best, for it saveth him best from the cross: and because he is of this carnal temper, therefore he seeketh to pervert my ways, though right. Now there are three things in this man's counsel that thou must utterly abhor.

*1 John 4:5*

*Galatians 6:12*

1. His turning thee out of the way.

2. His laboring to render the cross odious to thee.

3. And his setting thy feet in that way that leadeth unto the administration of death.

First, Thou must abhor his turning thee out of the way; yea, and thine own consenting thereto; because this is to reject the counsel of God for the sake of the counsel of a Worldly Wiseman. The Lord says, "Strive to enter in at the straight gate," the gate to which I send thee; "for strait is the gate that leadeth unto life, and few there be that find it." From this little wicket-gate, and from the way thereto, hath this wicked man turned thee, to the bringing of thee almost to destruction: hate, therefore, his turning thee out of the way, and abhor thyself for hearkening to him.

*Luke 13:24*

*Matthew 7:13–14*

Secondly, Thou must abhor his laboring to render the cross odious unto thee; for thou art to prefer it before the treasures of Egypt. Besides, the King of glory hath told thee, that he that will save his life shall lose it. And he that comes after him, and hates not his father, and mother, and wife, and children, and brethren, and sisters, yea, and his own life also, he cannot be his disciple. I say, therefore, for a man to labor to persuade thee that that shall be thy death, without which, the truth hath said, thou canst not have eternal life, this doctrine thou must abhor.

*Hebrews 11:25–26*

*Mark 8:38*
*John 12:25*
*Matthew 10:39*
*Luke 14:26*

Thirdly, Thou must hate his setting of thy feet in the way that leadeth to the ministration of death. And for this thou must consider to whom he sent thee, and also how unable that person was to deliver thee from thy burden.

He to whom thou wast sent for ease, being by name Legality, is the son of the bond-woman which now is, and is in bondage with her children, and is, in a mystery, this Mount Sinai, which thou hast feared will fall on thy head. Now if she with her children are in bondage, how canst thou expect by them to be made free? This Legality, therefore, is not able to set thee free from thy burden. No man was as yet ever rid of his burden by him; no, nor ever is like to be: ye cannot be justified by the works of the law; for by the deeds of the law no man living can be rid of his burden: Therefore Mr. Worldly Wiseman is an alien, and Mr. Legality is a cheat; and for his son Civility, notwithstanding his simpering looks, he is but a hypocrite, and cannot help thee. Believe me, there is nothing in all this noise that thou hast heard of these sottish men, but a design to beguile thee of thy salvation, by turning thee from the way in which I had set thee.

*Galatians 4:21–27*

After this, Evangelist called aloud to the heavens for confirmation of what he had said; and with that there came words and fire out of the mountain under which poor Christian stood, which made the hair of his flesh stand up. The words were pronounced: "As many as are of the works of the law, are under the curse; for it is written, Cursed is every one that continueth not in all things which are written in the book of the law to do them." *Galatians 3:10*

Now Christian looked for nothing but death, and began to cry out lamentably; even cursing the time in which he met with Mr. Worldly Wiseman; still calling himself a thousand fools for hearkening to his counsel. He also was greatly ashamed to think that this gentleman's arguments, flowing only from the flesh, should have the prevalency with him so far as to cause him to forsake the right way. This done, he applied himself again to Evangelist in words and sense as follows.

> CHRISTIAN: Sir, what think you? Is there any hope? May I now go back, and go up to the wicket-gate? Shall I not be abandoned for this, and sent back from thence ashamed? I am sorry I have hearkened to this man's counsel; but may my sin be forgiven?

> EVANGELIST: Then said Evangelist to him, Thy sin is very great, for by it thou hast committed two evils: thou hast forsaken the way that is good, to tread in forbidden paths. Yet will the man at the gate receive thee, for he has goodwill for men; only, said he, take heed that thou turn not aside again, lest thou "perish from the way, when his wrath is kindled but a little." *Psalm 2:12*

# 7

# GOODWILL

THEN DID Christian address himself to go back; and Evangelist, after he had kissed him, gave him one smile, and bid him God speed; So he went on with haste, neither spake he to any man by the way; nor if any asked him, would he vouchsafe them an answer. He went like one that was all the while treading on forbidden ground, and could by no means think himself safe, till again he was got into the way which he had left to follow Mr. Worldly Wiseman's counsel. So, in process of time, Christian got up to the gate. Now, over the gate there was written, "Knock, and it shall be opened unto you." *Matthew 7:7*

> He that will enter in must first without
> Stand knocking at the gate, nor need he doubt
> That as a knocker but to enter in
> For God can love him and forgive his sin.

He knocked, therefore, more than once or twice, saying,

> "May I now enter here? Will he within
> Open to sorry me, though I have been
> An undeserving rebel? Then shall I
> Not fail to sing his lasting praise on high."

At last there came a grave person to the gate, named Goodwill, who asked who was there, and whence he came, and what he would have.

CHRISTIAN: Here is a poor burdened sinner. I come from the city of Destruction, but am go-

ing to Mount Zion, that I may be delivered from the wrath to come; I would therefore, sir, since I am informed that by this gate is the way thither, know if you are willing to let me in.

GOODWILL: I am willing with all my heart, said he; and with that he opened the gate.

So when Christian was stepping in, the other gave him a pull. Then said Christian, What means that? The other told him, A little distance from this gate there is erected a strong castle, of which Beelzebub is the captain: from thence both he and they that are with him, shoot arrows at those that come up to this gate, if haply they may die before they can enter in. Then said Christian, I rejoice and tremble. So when he was got in, the man of the Gate asked him who directed him thither.

CHRISTIAN: Evangelist bid me come hither and knock, as I did: and he said, that you, sir, would tell me what I must do.

GOODWILL: An open door is set before thee, and no man can shut it.

CHRISTIAN: Now I begin to reap the benefits of my hazards.

GOODWILL: But how is it that you came alone?

CHRISTIAN: Because none of my neighbors saw their danger as I saw mine.

GOODWILL: Did any of them know of your coming?

CHRISTIAN: Yes, my wife and children saw me at the first, and called after me to turn again: also, some of my neighbors stood crying and calling after me to return; but I put my fingers in my ears, and so came on my way.

GOODWILL: But did none of them follow you, to persuade you to go back?

CHRISTIAN: Yes, both Obstinate and Pliable; but when they saw that they could not prevail, Obstinate went railing back; but Pliable came with me a little way.

GOODWILL: But why did he not come through?

CHRISTIAN: We indeed came both together

until we came to the Slough of Despond, into the which we also suddenly fell. And then was my neighbor Pliable discouraged, and would not venture farther. Wherefore, getting out again on the side next to his own house, he told me I should possess the brave country alone for him: so he went his way, and I came mine; he after Obstinate, and I to this gate.

GOODWILL: Then said Goodwill, Alas, poor man; is the celestial glory of so little esteem with him, that he counteth it not worth running the hazard of a few difficulties to obtain it?

CHRISTIAN: Truly, said Christian, I have said the truth of Pliable; and if I should also say all the truth of myself, it will appear there is no betterment betwixt him and myself. It is true, he went back to his own house, but I also turned aside to go in the way of death, being persuaded thereto by the carnal arguments of one Mr. Worldly Wiseman.

GOODWILL: Oh, did he light upon you? What, he would have had you have seek for ease at the hands of Mr. Legality! They are both of them a very cheat. But did you take his counsel?

CHRISTIAN: Yes, as far as I durst. I went to find out Mr. Legality, until I thought that the mountain that stands by his house would have fallen upon my head; wherefore there I was forced to stop.

GOODWILL: That mountain has been the death of many, and will be the death of many more: it is well you escaped being by it dashed in pieces.

CHRISTIAN: Why truly I do not know what

had become of me there, had not Evangelist happily met me again as I was musing in the midst of my dumps; but it was God's mercy that he came to me again, for else I had never come hither. But now I am come, such a one as I am, more fit indeed for death by that mountain, than thus to stand talking with my Lord. But O, what a favor is this to me, that yet I am admitted entrance here!

GOODWILL: We make no objections against any, notwithstanding all that they have done before they come hither; they in no wise are cast out. And therefore good Christian, come a little way with me, and I will teach thee about the way thou must go. Look before thee; dost thou see this narrow way? That is the way thou must go. It was cast up by the patriarchs, prophets, Christ, and his apostles, and it is as strait as a rule can make it; this is the way thou must go.

John 6:37

CHRISTIAN: But, said Christian, are there no turnings nor windings, by which a stranger may lose his way?

GOODWILL: Yes, there are many ways butt down upon this, and they are crooked and wide: but thus thou mayest distinguish the right from the wrong, the right only being strait and narrow.

Matthew 7:14

Then I saw in my dream that Christian asked him further, if he could not help him off with his burden that was upon his back. For as yet he had not got rid thereof; nor could he by any means get it off without help.

He told him, "As to thy burden, be content to bear it until thou comest to the place of deliverance; for there it will fall from thy back of itself."

Then Christian began to gird up his loins, and to

address himself to his journey. So the other told him, that by that he was gone some distance from the gate, he would come to the house of the Interpreter, at whose door he should knock, and he would show him excellent things. Then Christian took his leave of his friend, and he again bid him God speed.

# 8

# HOUSE OF THE INTERPRETER, PICTURE ON THE WALL, PARLOR OF DUST

THEN HE went on till he came at the house of the Interpreter, where he knocked over and over. At last one came to the door, and asked who was there.

CHRISTIAN: Sir, here is a traveller, who was bid by an acquaintance of the good man of this house to call here for my profit; I would therefore speak with the master of the house.

So he called for the master of the house, who, after a little time, came to Christian, and asked him what he would have.

CHRISTIAN: Sir, said Christian, I am a man that am come from the city of Destruction, and am going to the Mount Zion; and I was told by the man that stands at the gate at the head of this way, that if I called here you would show me excellent things, such as would be helpful to me on my journey.

INTERPRETER: Then said Interpreter, Come in; I will show thee that which will be profitable to thee. So he commanded his man to light the candle, and bid Christian follow him; so he had him into a private room, and bid his man open a door; the which when he had done, Christian saw the picture a very grave person hang up against the wall; and this was the fashion of it: It had eyes lifted up to heaven, the best of books in his hand, the law of truth was written upon its lips, the world was behind its back; it stood as if it pleaded with men, and a crown of gold did hang over its head.

CHRISTIAN: Then said Christian, What means this?

INTERPRETER: The man whose picture this is, is one of a thousand: he can beget children, travail in birth with children, and nurse them himself when they are born. And whereas thou seest him with his eyes lift up to heaven, the best of books in his hand, and the law of truth writ on his lips: it is to show thee, that his work is to know, and unfold dark things to sinners; even as also thou seest him stand as if he pleaded with men. And whereas thou seest the world as cast behind him, and that a crown hangs over his head; that is to show thee, that slighting and despising the things that are present, for the love that he hath to his Master's service, he is sure in the world that comes next, to have glory for his reward. Now, said the Interpreter, I have showed thee this picture first, because the man whose picture this is, is the only man whom the Lord of the place whither thou art going hath authorized to be thy guide in all difficult places thou mayest meet with in the way: wherefore take good heed to what I have showed thee, and bear well in thy mind what thou hast seen, lest in thy journey thou meet with some that pretend to lead thee right, but their way goes down to death.

*1 Corinthians 4:15*

*Galatians 4:19*

Then he took him by the hand, and led him into a very large parlor that was full of dust, because never

swept; the which after he had reviewed it a little while, the Interpreter called for a man to sweep. Now, when he began to sweep, the dust began so abundantly to fly about, that Christian had almost therewith been choked. Then said the Interpreter to a damsel that stood by, "Bring hither water, and sprinkle the room;" the which when she had done, it was swept and cleansed with pleasure.

CHRISTIAN: Then said Christian, What means this?

INTERPRETER: The Interpreter answered, This parlor is the heart of a man that was never sanctified by the sweet grace of the Gospel. The dust is his original sin, and inward corruptions, that have defiled the whole man. He that began to sweep at first, is the law; but she that brought water, and did sprinkle it, is the Gospel. Now whereas thou sawest, that so soon as the first began to sweep, the dust did so fly about that the room by him could not be cleansed, but that thou wast almost choked therewith; this is to show thee, that the law, instead of cleansing the heart (by its working) from sin, doth revive, put strength into, and increase it in the soul, even as it doth discover and forbid it; for it doth not give power to subdue. Again, as thou sawest the damsel sprinkle the room with water, upon which it was cleansed with pleasure, this is to show thee, that when the Gospel comes in the sweet and precious influences thereof to the heart, then, I say, even as thou sawest the damsel lay the dust by sprinkling the floor with water, so is sin vanquished and subdued, and the soul made clean, through the faith of it, and consequently fit for the King of glory to inhabit.

*Romans 7:9*

*1 Corinthians 15:56*
*Romans 5:20*

*John 15:3*
*Ephesians 5:26*
*Acts 15:9*
*Romans 16:25–26*

# 9

# PATIENCE & PASSION, FIRE ON THE WALL, VALIANT MAN

I SAW MOREOVER in my dream, that the Interpreter took him by the hand, and had him into a little room, where sat two little children, each one in his chair. The name of the eldest was Passion, and the name of the other Patience. Passion seemed to be much discontented, but Patience was very quiet. Then Christian asked, "What is the reason of the discontent of Passion?" The Interpreter answered, "The governor of them would have him stay for his best things till the beginning of the next year, but he will have all now; but Patience is willing to wait."

Then I saw that one came to Passion, and brought him a bag of treasure, and poured it down at his feet: the which he took up, and rejoiced therein, and withal laughed Patience to scorn. But I beheld but a while, and he had lavished all away, and had nothing left him but rags.

CHRISTIAN: Then said Christian to the Interpreter, Expound this matter more fully to me.

INTERPRETER: So he said, These two lads are

figures; Passion of the men of this world, and Patience of the men of that which is to come; for, as here thou seest, passion will have all now, this year, that is to say, in this world; so are the men of this world: They must have all their good things now; they cannot stay till the next year, that is, until the next world, for their portion of good. That proverb, "A bird in the hand is worth two in the bush," is of more authority with them

than are all the divine testimonies of the good of the world to come. But as thou sawest that he had quickly lavished all away, and had presently left him nothing but rags, so will it be with all such men at the end of this world.

CHRISTIAN: Then said Christian, Now I see that Patience has the best wisdom, and that upon many accounts. 1. Because he stays for the best things. 2. And also because he will have the glory of his, when the other has nothing but rags.

INTERPRETER: Nay, you may add another, to wit, the glory of the next world will never wear out; but these are suddenly gone. Therefore Passion had not so much reason to laugh at Patience because he had his good things first, as Patience will have to laugh at Passion because he had his best things last; for first must give place to last, because last must have his time to come: but last gives place to nothing, for there is not another to succeed. He, therefore, that hath his portion first, must needs have a time to spend it; but he that hath his portion last, must have it lastingly: therefore it is said of Dives, "In thy lifetime thou receivedst thy good things, and likewise Lazarus evil things; but now he is comforted, and thou art tormented."

*Luke 16:25*

CHRISTIAN: Then I perceive it is not best to covet things that are now, but to wait for things to come.

INTERPRETER: You say truth: for the things that are seen are temporal, but the things that are not seen are eternal. But though this be so, yet since things present and our fleshly appetite are such near neighbors one to another; and again,

*2 Corinthians 4:18*

because things to come and carnal sense are such strangers one to another; therefore it is, that the first of these so suddenly fall into amity, and that distance is so continued between the second.

Then I saw in my dream, that the Interpreter took Christian by the hand, and led him into a place where was a fire burning against a wall, and one standing by it, always casting much water upon it, to quench it; yet did the fire burn higher and hotter.

Then said Christian, What means this?

The Interpreter answered, This fire is the work of grace that is wrought in the heart; he that casts water upon it, to extinguish and put it out, is the devil: but in that thou seest the fire, notwithstanding, burn higher and hotter, thou shalt also see the reason of that. So he had him about to the back side of the wall, where he saw a man with a vessel of oil in his hand, of the which he did also continually cast (but secretly) into the fire.

Then said Christian, What means this?

The Interpreter answered, This is Christ, who continually, with the oil of his grace, maintains the work already begun in the heart; by the means of which, notwithstanding what the devil can do, the souls of his

2 Corinthians 12:9

people prove gracious still. And in that thou sawest that the man stood behind the wall to maintain the fire; this is to teach thee, that it is hard for the tempted to see how this work of grace is maintained in the soul.

I saw also, that the Interpreter took him again by the hand, and led him into a pleasant place, where was built a stately palace, beautiful to behold; at the sight of which Christian was greatly delighted. He saw also upon the top thereof certain persons walking, who were clothed all in gold.

Then said Christian may we go in thither?

Then the Interpreter took him, and led him up to-

wards the door of the palace; and behold, at the door stood a great company of men, as desirous to go in, but durst not. There also sat a man at a little distance from the door, at a table-side, with a book and his inkhorn before him, to take the names of them that should enter therein; he saw also that in the doorway stood many men in armor to keep it, being resolved to do to the men that would enter, what hurt and mischief they could. Now was Christian somewhat in amaze. At last, when

every man started back for fear of the armed men, Christian saw a man of a very stout countenance come up to the man that sat there to write, saying, "Set down my name, sir;" the which when he had done, he saw the man draw his sword, and put a helmet on his head, and rush towards the door upon the armed men, who laid upon him with deadly force; but the man, not at all discouraged, fell to cutting and hacking most fiercely. So after he had received and given many wounds to those that attempted to keep him out, he cut his way through them all, and pressed forward into the palace; at which there was a pleasant voice heard from those that were within, even of those that walked upon the top of the palace, saying,

*Matthew 11:12*
*Acts 14:22*

"Come in, come in, Eternal glory thou shalt win."

So he went in, and was clothed with such garments as they. Then Christian smiled, and said, I think verily I know the meaning of this.

Now, said Christian, let me go hence.

Nay, stay, said the Interpreter, till I have showed thee a little more, and after that thou shalt go on thy way.

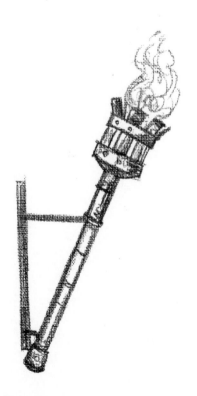

# 10

# Man in Iron Cage,
# Man with Dream

So HE took him by the hand again, and led him into a very dark room, where there sat a man in an iron cage.

Now the man, to look on, seemed very sad; he sat with his eyes looking down to the ground, his hands folded together, and he sighed as if he would break his heart. Then said Christian, What means this? At which the Interpreter bid him talk with the man.

Then said Christian to the man, What art thou? The man answered, I am what I was not once.

CHRISTIAN: What wast thou once?

THE MAN: The man said, I was once a fair and flourishing professor, both in mine own eyes, and also in the eyes of others: I once was, as I thought, fair for the celestial city, and had then even joy at the thoughts that I should get thither.

*Luke 8:13*

CHRISTIAN: Well, but what art thou now?

THE MAN: I am now a man of despair, and am shut up in it, as in this iron cage. I cannot get out; Oh now I cannot!

CHRISTIAN: But how camest thou into this condition?

THE MAN: I left off to watch and be sober: I laid the reins upon the neck of my lusts; I sinned against the light of the word, and the goodness of God; I have grieved the Spirit, and he is gone; I tempted the devil, and he is come to me; I have provoked God to anger, and he has left me: I have so hardened my heart, that I cannot repent.

Then said Christian to the Interpreter, But is there

no hope for such a man as this? Ask him, said the Interpreter.

CHRISTIAN: Then said Christian, Is there no hope, but you must be kept in the iron cage of despair?

THE MAN: No, none at all.

CHRISTIAN: Why, the Son of the Blessed is very pitiful.

THE MAN: I have crucified him to myself afresh; I have despised his person; I have despised his righteousness; I have counted his blood an unholy thing; I have done despite to the spirit of grace: therefore I have shut myself out of all the promises and there now remains to me nothing but threatenings, dreadful threatenings, faithful threatenings of certain judgment and fiery indignation, which shall devour me as an adversary.

*Hebrews 6:6*

*Luke 19:14*

*Hebrews 10:29*

CHRISTIAN: For what did you bring yourself into this condition?

THE MAN: For the lusts, pleasures, and profits of this world; in the enjoyment of which I did then promise myself much delight: but now every one of those things also bite me, and gnaw me like a burning worm.

CHRISTIAN: But canst thou not now repent and turn?

THE MAN: God hath denied me repentance. His word gives me no encouragement to believe; yea, himself hath shut me up in this iron cage: nor can all the men in the world let me out. Oh eternity! eternity! how shall I grapple with the misery that I must meet with in eternity?

INTERPRETER: Then said the Interpreter to Christian, Let this man's misery be remembered by thee, and be an everlasting caution to thee.

CHRISTIAN: Well, said Christian, this is fearful! God help me to watch and to be sober, and to pray that I may shun the cause of this man's misery. Sir, is it not time for me to go on my way now?

INTERPRETER: Tarry till I shall show thee one thing more, and then thou shalt go on thy way.

So he took Christian by the hand again and led him into a chamber where there was one rising out of bed; and as he put on his raiment, he shook and trembled. Then said Christian, Why doth this man thus tremble? The Interpreter then bid him tell to Christian the reason of his so doing.

So he began, and said, "This night, as I was in my sleep, I dreamed, and behold the heavens grew exceeding black; also it thundered and lightened in most fearful wise, that it put me into an agony. So I looked up in my dream, and saw the clouds rack at an unusual rate; upon which I heard a great sound of a trumpet, and saw also a man sitting upon a cloud, attended with the thousands of heaven: they were all in flaming fire; also the heavens were in a burning flame. I heard then a voice, saying, 'Arise, ye dead, and come to judgment.' And with that the rocks rent, the graves opened, and the dead that were therein came forth: some of them were exceeding glad, and looked upward; and some sought to hide themselves under the mountains. Then I saw the man that sat upon the cloud open the book, and bid the world draw near. Yet there was, by reason of a fierce flame that issued out and came from before him, a convenient distance between him and them, as between the judge and the

*1 Corinthians 15*
*1 Thessalonians*
*4:16*
*Jude 15*
*John 5:28–29*
*2 Thessalonians*
*1:8–10*
*Revelation*
*20:11–14*
*Isaiah 26:21*
*Micah 7:16–17*
*Psalm 5:4;*
*50:1–3*
*Malachi 3:2–3*
*Daniel 7:9–10*

prisoners at the bar.

"I heard it also proclaimed to them that attended on the man that sat on the cloud, 'Gather together the tares, the chaff, and stubble, and cast them into the burning lake.' And with that the bottomless pit opened, just whereabout I stood; out of the mouth of which there came, in an abundant manner, smoke, and coals of fire, with hideous noises. It was also said to the same persons, 'Gather my wheat into the garner.' And with that I saw

*Matthew 3:12;*
*18:30;*
*24:30*
*Malachi 4:1*

*Luke 3:17*

*1 Thessalonians
4:16–17*

*Romans 2:14–15*

many catched up and carried away into the clouds, but I was left behind. I also sought to hide myself, but I could not, for the man that sat upon the cloud still kept his eye upon me; my sins also came into my mind, and my conscience did accuse me on every side. Upon this I awakened from my sleep."

CHRISTIAN: But what was it that made you so afraid of this sight?

THE MAN: Why, I thought that the day of judgment was come, and that I was not ready for it: but this frightened me most, that the angels gathered up several, and left me behind; also the pit of hell opened her mouth just where I stood. My conscience too afflicted me; and, as I thought, the Judge had always his eye upon me, showing indignation in his countenance.

# 11

# SALVATION

T HEN SAID the Interpreter to Christian, "Hast thou considered all these things?"

CHRISTIAN: Yes, and they put me in hope and fear.

INTERPRETER: Well, keep all things so in thy mind, that they may be as a goad in thy sides, to prick thee forward in the way thou must go. Then Christian began to gird up his loins, and to address himself to his journey. Then said the Interpreter, "The Comforter be always with thee, good Christian, to guide thee in the way that leads to the city." So Christian went on his way, saying,

"Here I have seen things rare and profitable,
Things pleasant, dreadful, things to make me stable
In what I have begun to take in hand:
Then let me think on them, and understand
Wherefore they showed me were, and let me be
Thankful, O good Interpreter, to thee."

Now I saw in my dream, that the highway up which Christian was to go, was fenced on either side with a wall, and that wall was called Salvation. Up this way, therefore, did burdened Christian run, but not without great difficulty, because of the load on his back.

*Isaiah 26:1*

He ran thus till he came at a place somewhat ascending; and upon that place stood a cross, and a little

below, in the bottom, a sepulchre. So I saw in my dream, that just as Christian came up with the cross, his burden loosed from off his shoulders, and fell from off his back, and began to tumble, and so continued to do till it came to the mouth of the sepulchre, where it fell in, and I saw it no more.

Then was Christian glad and lightsome, and said with a merry heart, "He hath given me rest by his sorrow, and life by his death." Then he stood still a while, to look and wonder; for it was very surprising to him that the sight of the cross should thus ease him of his burden. He looked, therefore, and looked again, even till the springs that were in his head sent the waters down his cheeks. Now as he stood looking and weeping, behold, three Shining Ones came to him, and saluted him with, "Peace be to thee." So the first said to him, "Thy sins be forgiven thee,"; the second stripped him of his rags, and clothed him with change of raiment; the third also set a mark on his forehead, and gave him a roll with a seal upon it, which he bid him look on as he ran, and that he should give it in at the celestial gate: so they went their way. Then Christian gave three leaps for joy, and went on singing,

*Zechariah 12:10*

*Mark 2:5*

*Ephesians 1:13*
*Zechariah 3:4*

> "Thus far did I come laden with my sin,
> Nor could aught ease the grief that I was in,
> Till I came hither. What a place is this!
> Must here be the beginning of my bliss?
> Must here the burden fall from off my back?
> Must here the strings that bound it to me crack?
> Blest cross! blest sepulchre! blest rather be
> The Man that there was put to shame for me!"

I saw then in my dream, that he went on thus, even until he came at the bottom, where he saw, a little out of the way, three men fast asleep, with fetters upon their heels. The name of the one was Simple, of another Sloth, and of the third Presumption.

Christian then seeing them lie in this case, went to them, if peradventure he might awake them, and cried, you are like them that sleep on the top of a mast, for the Dead Sea is under you, a gulf that hath no bottom: awake, therefore, and come away; be willing also, and I will help you off with your irons. He also told them, If he that goeth about like a roaring lion comes by, you will certainly become a prey to his teeth. With that they looked upon him, and began to reply in this sort: Simple

*Proverbs 23:34*

*1 Peter 5:8*

said, I see no danger; Sloth said, Yet a little more sleep; and Presumption said, Every tub must stand upon its own bottom. And so they lay down to sleep again, and Christian went on his way.

Yet he was troubled to think that men in that danger should so little esteem the kindness of him that so freely offered to help them, both by awakening of them, counselling of them, and proffering to help them off with their irons.

# 12

# FORMALIST & HYPOCRISY

AND AS he was troubled thereabout, he espied two men come tumbling over the wall, on the left hand of the narrow way; and they made up apace to him. The name of the one was Formalist, and the name of the other Hypocrisy. So, as I said, they drew up unto him, who thus entered with them into discourse.

CHRISTIAN: Gentlemen, whence came you, and whither do you go?

FORMALIST AND HYPOCRISY: We were born in the land of Vain-glory, and are going, for praise, to Mount Zion.

CHRISTIAN: Why came you not in at the gate which standeth at the beginning of the way? Know ye not that it is written, that "he that cometh not in by the door, but climbeth up some other way, the same is a thief and a robber?"

*John 10:1*

FORMALIST AND HYPOCRISY: They said, that to go to the gate for entrance was by all their countrymen counted too far about; and that therefore their usual way was to make a short cut of it, and to climb over the wall, as they had done.

CHRISTIAN: But will it not be counted a trespass against the Lord of the city whither we are bound, thus to violate his revealed will?

FORMALIST AND HYPOCRISY: They told him, that as for that, he needed not to trouble his head thereabout: for what they did they had custom for, and could produce, if need were, testimony that would witness it for more than a thousand years.

CHRISTIAN: But, said Christian, will you stand a trial at law?

FORMALIST AND HYPOCRISY: They told him, that custom, it being of so long standing as above a thousand years, would doubtless now be admitted as a thing legal by an impartial judge: and besides, said they, if we get into the way, what matter is it which way we get in? If we are in, we are in: thou art but in the way, who, as we perceive, came in at the gate; and we also are in the way, that came tumbling over the wall: wherein now is thy condition better than ours?

CHRISTIAN: I walk by the rule of my Master: you walk by the rude working of your fancies. You are counted thieves already by the Lord of the way: therefore I doubt you will not be found true men at the end of the way. You come in by yourselves without his direction, and shall go out by yourselves without his mercy.

To this they made him but little answer; only they bid him look to himself. Then I saw that they went on, every man in his way, without much conference one with another, save that these two men told Christian, that as to laws and ordinances, they doubted not but that they should as conscientiously do them as he. Therefore, said they, we see not wherein thou differest from us, but by the coat that is on thy back, which was, as we trow, given thee by some of thy neighbors, to hide the shame of thy nakedness.

CHRISTIAN: By laws and ordinances you will not be saved, since you came not in by the door. And as for this coat that is on my back, it was given me by the Lord of the place whither I go; and that, as you say, to cover my nakedness with.

*Galatians 2:16*

And I take it as a token of kindness to me; for I
had nothing but rags before. And besides, thus I
comfort myself as I go. Surely, think I, when I
come to the gate of the city, the Lord thereof
will know me for good, since I have his coat on
my back; a coat that he gave me freely in the day
that he stripped me of my rags. I have, moreover, a mark in my forehead, of which perhaps
you have taken no notice, which one of my

Lord's most intimate associates fixed there in the day that my burden fell off my shoulders. I will tell you, moreover, that I had then given me a roll sealed, to comfort me by reading as I go on the way; I was also bid to give it in at the celestial gate, in token of my certain going in after it: all which things I doubt you want, and want them because you came not in at the gate.

To these things they gave him no answer; only they looked upon each other, and laughed. Then I saw that they went all on, save that Christian kept before, who had no more talk but with himself, and that sometimes sighingly, and sometimes comfortably: also he would be often reading in the roll that one of the Shining Ones gave him, by which he was refreshed.

I beheld then, that they all went on till they came to the foot of the hill Difficulty, at the bottom of which there was a spring. There were also in the same place two other ways besides that which came straight from the gate: one turned to the left hand, and the other to the right, at the bottom of the hill; but the narrow way lay right up the hill, and the name of the going up the side of the hill is called Difficulty. Christian now went to the spring, and drank thereof to refresh himself, and *Isaiah 49:10* then began to go up the hill, saying,

"The hill, though high, I covet to ascend;
The difficulty will not me offend;
For I perceive the way to life lies here:
Come, pluck up heart, let's neither faint nor fear.
Better, though *difficult*, the right way to go,
Than wrong, though *easy*, where the end is woe."

The other two also came to the foot of the hill. But when they saw that the hill was steep and high, and that there were two other ways to go; and supposing also that these two ways might meet again with that up which Christian went, on the other side of the hill; therefore they were resolved to go in those ways. Now the name of one of those ways was Danger, and the name of the other Destruction. So the one took the way which is called Danger, which led him into a great wood; and the other took directly up the way to Destruction, which led him into a wide field, full of dark mountains, where he stumbled and fell, and rose no more.

# 13

# TIMOROUS & MISTRUST

I LOOKED THEN after Christian, to see him go up the hill, where I perceived he fell from running to going, and from going to clambering upon his hands and his knees, because of the steepness of the place. Now about the midway to the top of the hill was a pleasant Arbor, made by the Lord of the hill for the refreshment of weary travellers. Thither, therefore, Christian got, where also he sat down to rest him: then he pulled his roll out of his bosom, and read therein to his comfort; he also now began afresh to take a review of the coat or garment that was given to him as he stood by the cross. Thus pleasing himself awhile, he at last fell into a slumber, and thence into a fast sleep, which detained him in that place until it was almost night; and in his sleep his roll fell out of his hand. Now, as he was sleeping, there came one to him, and awaked him, saying, "Go to the ant, thou sluggard; consider her ways, and be wise." And with that, Christian suddenly started up, and sped him on his way, and went apace till he came to the top of the hill.

*Proverbs 6:6*

Now when he was got up to the top of the hill, there came two men running amain; the name of the one was Timorous, and of the other Mistrust: to whom Christian said, Sirs, what's the matter? you run the wrong way. Timorous answered, that they were going to the city of Zion, and had got up that difficult place: but, said he, the farther we go, the more danger we meet with; wherefore we turned, and are going back again.

Yes, said Mistrust, for just before us lie a couple of lions in the way, whether sleeping or waking we know not; and we could not think, if we came within reach, but they would presently pull us in pieces.

CHRISTIAN: Then said Christian, You make me afraid; but whither shall I fly to be safe? If I go back to mine own country, that is prepared for fire and brimstone, and I shall certainly perish there; if I can get to the celestial city, I am sure to be in safety there: I must venture. To go back is nothing but death: to go forward is fear of death, and life everlasting beyond it: I will yet go forward.

So Mistrust and Timorous ran down the hill, and Christian went on his way. But thinking again of what he had heard from the men, he felt in his bosom for his roll, that he might read therein and be comforted; but he felt, and found it not. Then was Christian in great distress, and knew not what to do; for he wanted that which used to relieve him, and that which should have been his pass into the celestial city. Here, therefore, he began to be much perplexed, and knew not what to do. At last he bethought himself that he had slept in the arbor that is on the side of the hill; and falling down upon his knees, he asked God forgiveness for that foolish act, and then went back to look for his roll. But all the way he went back, who can sufficiently set forth the sorrow of Christian's heart? Sometimes he sighed, sometimes he wept, and oftentimes he chid himself for being so foolish to fall asleep in that place, which was erected only for a little refreshment from his weariness. Thus, therefore, he went back, carefully looking on this side and on that, all the way as he went, if happily he might find his roll, that had been his comfort so many times in his journey. He went thus till he came again in sight of the arbor where he sat and slept; but that sight renewed his sorrow the more, by bringing again, even afresh, his evil of sleeping unto his mind. Thus, therefore, he now went on, bewailing his sinful sleep, saying, O wretched man that I am, that I should sleep in the daytime! that I should sleep in the midst of difficulty! that I should so indulge the flesh as to use that rest for ease to my flesh which the Lord of the hill hath erected only for the relief of the spirits of pilgrims! How many steps have I

*Revelation 2:4*
*1 Thessalonians 5:6–8*

taken in vain! Thus it happened to Israel; for their sin they were sent back again by the way of the Red Sea; and I am made to tread those steps with sorrow, which I might have trod with delight, had it not been for this sinful sleep. How far might I have been on my way by this time! I am made to tread those steps thrice over, which I needed not to have trod but once: yea, now also I am like to be benighted, for the day is almost spent. O that I had not slept!

# 14

# PORTER & DISCRETION

NOW BY this time he was come to the arbor
again, where for a while he sat down and wept;
but at last, (as Christian would have it,) looking sorrow-
fully down under the settle, there he espied his roll, the
which he with trembling and haste catched up, and put
it into his bosom. But who can tell how joyful this man
was when he had gotten his roll again? For this roll was
the assurance of his life, and acceptance at the desired
haven. Therefore he laid it up in his bosom, gave thanks
to God for directing his eye to the place where it lay, and
with joy and tears betook himself again to his journey.

But O how nimbly did he go up the rest of the hill!
Yet before he got up, the sun went down upon Christian;
and this made him again recall the vanity of his sleeping
to his remembrance; and thus he again began to condole
with himself: Oh thou sinful sleep! how for thy sake am I
like to be benighted in my journey! I must walk without
the sun, darkness must cover the path of my feet, and I
must hear the noise of the doleful creatures, because of
my sinful sleep!

Now also he remembered the story that Mistrust
and Timorous told him of, how they were frighted with
the sight of the lions. Then said Christian to himself
again, These beasts range in the night for their prey; and
if they should meet with me in the dark, how should
I shift them? how should I escape being by them torn
in pieces? Thus he went on his way. But while he was
bewailing his unhappy miscarriage, he lift up his eyes,

and behold there was a very stately palace before him, the name of which was Beautiful, and it stood by the highway-side.

So I saw in my dream that he made haste, and went forward, that if possible he might get lodging there. Now before he had gone far, he entered into a very narrow passage, which was about a furlong off the Porter's lodge, and looking very narrowly before him as he went, he espied two lions in the way. Now, thought he, I see the dangers that Mistrust and Timorous were driven back by. (The lions were chained, but he saw not the chains.) Then he was afraid, and thought also himself to go back after them; for he thought nothing but death was before him. But the Porter at the lodge, whose name is Watchful, perceiving that Christian made a halt, as if he would go back, cried unto him, saying, Is thy strength so small? Fear not the lions, for they are chained, and are placed there for trial of faith where it is, and for discovery of those that have none: keep in the midst of the path, and no hurt shall come unto thee.

*Mark 4:40*

Then I saw that he went on, trembling for fear of the lions, but taking good heed to the directions of the Porter; he heard them roar, but they did him no harm. Then he clapped his hands, and went on till he came and stood before the gate where the Porter was. Then said Christian to the Porter, Sir, what house is this? and may I lodge here to-night? The Porter answered, This house was built by the Lord of the hill, and he built it for the relief and security of pilgrims. The Porter also asked whence he was, and whither he was going.

CHRISTIAN: I am come from the city of Destruction, and am going to Mount Zion: but because the sun is now set, I desire, if I may, to lodge here to-night.

THE PORTER: What is your name?

CHRISTIAN: My name is now Christian, but my name at the first was Graceless: I came of the race of Japheth, whom God will persuade to dwell in the tents of Shem.

*Genesis 9:27*

THE PORTER: But how does it happen that you come so late? The sun is set.

CHRISTIAN: I had been here sooner, but that,

wretched man that I am, I slept in the arbor that stands on the hill-side! Nay, I had, notwithstanding that, been here much sooner, but that in my sleep I lost my evidence, and came without it to the brow of the hill; and then feeling for it, and not finding it, I was forced with sorrow of heart to go back to the place where I slept my sleep, where I found it; and now I am come.

THE PORTER: Well, I will call out one of the virgins of this place, who will, if she likes your talk, bring you in to the rest of the family, according to the rules of the house. So Watchful the Porter rang a bell, at the sound of which came out of the door of the house a grave and beautiful damsel, named Discretion, and asked why she was called.

The Porter answered, This man is on a journey from the city of Destruction to Mount Zion; but being weary and benighted, he asked me if he might lodge here to-night: so I told him I would call for thee, who, after discourse had with him, mayest do as seemeth thee good, even according to the law of the house.

Then she asked him whence he was, and whither he was going; and he told her. She asked him also how he got into the way; and he told her. Then she asked him what he had seen and met with in the way, and he told her. And at last she asked his name. So he said, It is Christian; and I have so much the more a desire to lodge here to-night, because, by what I perceive, this place was built by the Lord of the hill for the relief and security of pilgrims. So she smiled, but the water stood in her eyes; and after a little pause she said, I will call forth two or three more of the family. So she ran to the door, and called out Prudence, Piety, and Charity, who, after a little more discourse with him, had him into the family; and many of them meeting him at the threshold of the house, said, Come in, thou blessed of the Lord; this house was built by the Lord of the hill on purpose to entertain such pilgrims in. Then he bowed his head, and followed them into the house. So when he was come in and sat down, they gave him something to drink, and consented together that, until supper was ready, some of them should have some particular discourse with Christian, for the best improvement of time; and they appointed Piety, Prudence, and Charity to discourse with him: and thus they began.

# 15

# PIETY, PRUDENCE,
# CHARITY

PIETY: COME, good Christian, since we have been so loving to you as to receive you into our house this night, let us, if perhaps we may better ourselves thereby, talk with you of all things that have happened to you in your pilgrimage.

CHRISTIAN: With a very good will; and I am glad that you are so well disposed.

PIETY: What moved you at first to betake yourself to a pilgrim's life?

CHRISTIAN: I was driven out of my native country by a dreadful sound that was in mine ears; to wit, that unavoidable destruction did attend me, if I abode in that place where I was.

PIETY: But how did it happen that you came out of your country this way?

CHRISTIAN: It was as God would have it; for when I was under the fears of destruction, I did not know whither to go; but by chance there came a man, even to me, as I was trembling and weeping, whose name is Evangelist, and he directed me to the Wicket-gate, which else I should never have found, and so set me into the way that hath led me directly to this house.

PIETY: But did you not come by the house of the Interpreter?

CHRISTIAN: Yes, and did see such things there, the remembrance of which will stick by me as long as I live, especially three things: to wit, how Christ, in despite of Satan, maintains his work of grace in the heart; how the man had sinned himself quite out of hopes of God's mercy; and also the dream of him that thought in his sleep the day of judgment was come.

PIETY: Why, did you hear him tell his dream?

CHRISTIAN: Yes, and a dreadful one it was, I thought; it made my heart ache as he was telling of it, but yet I am glad I heard it.

PIETY: Was this all you saw at the house of the Interpreter?

CHRISTIAN: No; he took me, and had me where he showed me a stately palace, and how the people were clad in gold that were in it; and how there came a venturous man, and cut his way through the armed men that stood in the door to keep him out; and how he was bid to come in, and win eternal glory. Methought those things did ravish my heart. I would have stayed at that good man's house a twelvemonth, but that I knew I had farther to go.

PIETY: And what saw you else in the way?

CHRISTIAN: Saw? Why, I went but a little farther, and I saw One, as I thought in my mind, hang bleeding upon a tree; and the very sight of him made my burden fall off my back; for I groaned under a very heavy burden, but then it fell down from off me. It was a strange thing to me, for I never saw such a thing before: yea, and while I stood looking up, (for then I could not forbear looking,) three Shining Ones came to me. One of them testified that my sins were forgiven me; another stripped me of my rags, and gave me this broidered coat which you see; and the third set the mark which you see in my forehead, and gave me this sealed roll, (and with that he plucked it out of his bosom.)

PIETY: But you saw more than this, did you not?

CHRISTIAN: The things that I have told you were the best: yet some other I saw, as, namely, I saw three men, Simple, Sloth, and Presumption, lie asleep, a little out of the way, as I came, with irons upon their heels; but do you think I could awake them? I also saw Formality and Hypocrisy come tumbling over the wall, to go, as they pretended, to Zion; but they were quickly lost, even as I myself did tell them, but they would not believe. But, above all, I found it hard work to get up this hill, and as hard to come by the lions' mouths; and, truly, if it had not been for the good man, the porter that stands at the gate, I do not know but that, after all, I might have gone back again; but I thank God I am here, and thank you for receiving me.

Then Prudence thought good to ask him a few questions, and desired his answer to them.

PRUDENCE: Do you not think sometimes of the country from whence you came?

CHRISTIAN: Yea, but with much shame and detestation. Truly, if I had been mindful of that country from whence I came out, I might have had opportunity to have returned; but now I desire a better country, that is, a heavenly one.

*Hebrews 11:15–16*

PRUDENCE: Do you not yet bear away with you some of the things that then you were conversant withal?

CHRISTIAN: Yes, but greatly against my will; especially my inward and carnal cogitations, with which all my countrymen, as well as myself, were delighted. But now all those things are my grief; and might I but choose mine own things, I would choose never to think of those things more: but when I would be a doing that which is best, that which is worst is with me.

*Romans 7:15, 21*

PRUDENCE: Do you not find sometimes as if those things were vanquished, which at other times are your perplexity?

CHRISTIAN: Yes, but that is but seldom; but they are to me golden hours in which such things happen to me.

PRUDENCE: Can you remember by what means you find your annoyances at times as if they were vanquished?

CHRISTIAN: Yes: when I think what I saw at the cross, that will do it; and when I look upon my broidered coat, that will do it; and when I look into the roll that I carry in my bosom, that will do it; and when my thoughts wax warm about whither I am going, that will do it.

PRUDENCE: And what is it that makes you so

desirous to go to Mount Zion?

CHRISTIAN: Why, there I hope to see Him alive that did hang dead on the cross; and there I hope to be rid of all those things that to this day are in me an annoyance to me: there they say there is no death, and there I shall dwell with such company as I like best. For, to tell you the truth, I love Him because I was by Him eased of my burden; and I am weary of my inward sickness. I would fain be where I shall die no more, and with the company that shall continually cry, Holy, holy, holy.

*Isaiah 25:8*
*Revelation 21:4*

Then said Charity to Christian, Have you a family; Are you a married man?

CHRISTIAN: I have a wife and four small children.

CHARITY: And why did you not bring them along with you?

CHRISTIAN: Then Christian wept, and said, Oh, how willingly would I have done it! but they were all of them utterly averse to my going on pilgrimage.

CHARITY: But you should have talked to them, and have endeavored to show them the danger of staying behind.

CHRISTIAN: So I did; and told them also what God had shown to me of the destruction of our city; but I seemed to them as one that mocked, and they believed me not.

*Genesis 19:14*

CHARITY: And did you pray to God that he would bless your counsel to them?

CHRISTIAN: Yes, and that with much affection; for you must think that my wife and poor children were very dear to me.

CHARITY: But did you tell them of your own sorrow, and fear of destruction? for I suppose that destruction was visible enough to you.

CHRISTIAN: Yes, over, and over, and over. They might also see my fears in my countenance, in my tears, and also in my trembling under the apprehension of the judgment that did hang over our heads; but all was not sufficient to prevail with them to come with me.

CHARITY: But what could they say for themselves, why they came not?

CHRISTIAN: Why, my wife was afraid of losing this world, and my children were given to the foolish delights of youth; so, what by one thing, and what by another, they left me to wander in this manner alone.

CHARITY: But did you not, with your vain life, damp all that you, by words, used by way of persuasion to bring them away with you?

CHRISTIAN: Indeed, I cannot commend my life, for I am conscious to myself of many failings therein. I know also, that a man, by his conversation, may soon overthrow what, by argument or persuasion, he doth labor to fasten upon others for their good. Yet this I can say, I was very wary of giving them occasion, by any unseemly action, to make them averse to going on pilgrimage. Yea, for this very thing, they would tell me I was too precise, and that I denied myself of things (for their sakes) in which they saw no evil. Nay, I think I may say, that if what they saw in me did hinder them, it was my great tenderness in sinning against God, or of doing any wrong to my neighbor.

CHARITY: Indeed, Cain hated his brother, because his own works were evil, and his brother's righteous; and if thy wife and children have been offended with thee for this, they thereby show themselves to be implacable to good; thou hast delivered thy soul from their blood.

*1 John 3:12*

*Ezekiel 3:19*

# 16

# PEACE IN THE PALACE

N OW I saw in my dream, that thus they sat talking together until supper was ready. So when they had made ready, they sat down to meat. Now the table was furnished with fat things, and with wine that was well refined; and all their talk at the table was about the Lord of the hill; as, namely, about what he had done, and wherefore he did what he did, and why he had builded that house; and by what they said, I perceived that he had been a great warrior, and had fought with and slain him that had the power of death,  but not without great danger to himself, which made me love him the more.

Hebrews 2:14–15

For, as they said, and as I believe, said Christian, he did it with the loss of much blood. But that which put the glory of grace into all he did, was, that he did it out of pure love to his country. And besides, there were some of them of the household that said they had been and spoke with him since he did die on the cross; and they have attested that they had it from his own lips, that he is such a lover of poor pilgrims, that the like is not to be found from the east to the west. They, more-over, gave an instance of what they affirmed; and that was, he had stripped himself of his glory that he might do this for the poor; and that they heard him say and affirm, that he would not dwell in the mountain of Zion alone. They said, moreover, that he had made many pil-grims princes, though by nature they were beggars born, and their original had been the dunghill.

1 Samuel 2:8<br>Psalm 113:7

Thus they discoursed together till late at night; and

after they had committed themselves to their Lord for protection, they betook themselves to rest. The pilgrim they laid in a large upper chamber, whose window opened towards the sun-rising. The name of the chamber was Peace, where he slept till break of day, and then he awoke and sang,

"Where am I now? Is this the love and care
Of Jesus, for the men that pilgrims are,
Thus to provide that I should be forgiven,
And dwell already the next door to heaven!"

So in the morning they all got up; and, after some more discourse, they told him that he should not depart till they had shown him the rarities of that place. And first they had him into the study, where they showed him records of the greatest antiquity; in which, as I remember my dream, they showed him the pedigree of the Lord of the hill, that he was the Son of the Ancient of days, and came by eternal generation. Here also was more fully recorded the acts that he had done, and the names of many hundreds that he had taken into his service; and how he had placed them in such habitations that could neither by length of days, nor decays of nature, be dissolved.

Then they read to him some of the worthy acts that some of his servants had done; as how they had subdued kingdoms, wrought righteousness, obtained promises, stopped the mouths of lions, quenched the violence of fire, escaped the edge of the sword, out of weakness were made strong, waxed valiant in fight, and turned to flight the armies of the aliens.

*Hebrews 11:33–34*

Then they read again another part of the records of the house, where it was shown how willing their Lord was to receive into his favor any, even any, though they in time past had offered great affronts to his person and proceedings. Here also were several other histories of many

other famous things, of all which Christian had a view; as of things both ancient and modern, together with prophecies and predictions of things that have their certain accomplishment, both to the dread and amazement of enemies, and the comfort and solace of pilgrims.

The next day they took him, and had him into the armory, where they showed him all manner of furniture which their Lord had provided for pilgrims, as sword, shield, helmet, breastplate, all-prayer, and shoes that would not wear out. And there was here enough of this to harness out as many men for the service of their Lord as there be stars in the heaven for multitude.

They also showed him some of the engines with which some of his servants had done wonderful things. They showed him Moses' rod; the hammer and nail with which Jael slew Sisera; the pitchers, trumpets, and lamps too, with which Gideon put to flight the armies of Midian. Then they showed him the ox-goad wherewith Shamgar slew six hundred men. They showed him also the jawbone with which Samson did such mighty feats. They showed him moreover the sling and stone with which David slew Goliath of Gath; and the sword also with which their Lord will kill the man of sin, in the day that he shall rise up to the prey. They showed him besides many excellent things, with which Christian was much delighted. This done, they went to their rest again.

Then I saw in my dream, that on the morrow he got up to go forward, but they desired him to stay till the next day also; and then, said they, we will, if the day be clear, show you the Delectable Mountains; which, they said, would yet farther add to his comfort, because they were nearer the desired haven than the place where at present he was; so he consented and stayed. When the morning was up, they had him to the top of the house, and bid him look south. So he did, and behold, at a great distance, he saw a most pleasant mountainous country, beautified with woods, vineyards, fruits of all sorts, flowers also, with springs and fountains, very delectable to *Isaiah 33:16–17* behold. Then he asked the name of the country. They said it was Immanuel's land; and it is as common, said they, as this hill is, to and for all the pilgrims. And when thou comest there, from thence thou mayest see to the gate of the celestial city, as the shepherds that live there will make appear.

Now he bethought himself of setting forward, and

they were willing he should. But first, said they, let us go again into the armory. So they did; and when he came there, they harnessed him from head to foot with what was of proof, lest perhaps he should meet with assaults in the way. He being therefore thus accoutred, walked out with his friends to the gate; and there he asked the Porter if he saw any pilgrim pass by. Then the Porter answered, Yes.

CHRISTIAN: Pray, did you know him? said he.

THE PORTER: I asked his name, and he told me it was Faithful.

CHRISTIAN: O, said Christian, I know him; he is my townsman, my near neighbor; he comes from the place where I was born. How far do you think he may be before?

THE PORTER: He is got by this time below the hill.

CHRISTIAN: Well, said Christian, good Porter, the Lord be with thee, and add to all thy plain blessings much increase for the kindness that thou hast showed me.

Then he began to go forward; but Discretion, Piety, Charity, and Prudence would accompany him down to the foot of the hill. So they went on together, reiterating their former discourses, till they came to go down the hill. Then said Christian, As it was difficult coming up, so, so far as I can see, it is dangerous going down. Yes, said Prudence, so it is; for it is a hard matter for a man to go down into the valley of Humiliation, as thou art now, and to catch no slip by the way; therefore, said they, we are come out to accompany thee down the hill. So he began to go down, but very warily; yet he caught a slip or two.

Then I saw in my dream, that these good companions, when Christian was got down to the bottom of the hill, gave him a loaf of bread, a bottle of wine, and a cluster of raisins; and then he went on his way,

"Whilst Christian is among his godly friends,
Their golden mouths make him sufficient mends
For all his griefs; and when they let him go,
He's clad with northern steel from top to toe."

# 17

# BATTLE WITH

# APOLLYON

BUT NOW, in this valley of Humiliation, poor Christian was hard put to it; for he had gone but a little way before he espied a foul fiend coming over the field to meet him: his name is Apollyon. Then did Christian begin to be afraid, and to cast in his mind whether to go back, or to stand his ground. But he considered again, that he had no armor for his back, and therefore thought that to turn the back to him might give him greater advantage with ease to pierce him with his darts; therefore he resolved to venture and stand his ground: for, thought he, had I no more in mine eye than the saving of my life, it would be the best way to stand.

So he went on, and Apollyon met him. Now the monster was hideous to behold: he was clothed with scales like a fish, and they are his pride; he had wings like a dragon, and feet like a bear, and out of his belly came fire and smoke; and his mouth was as the mouth of a lion. When he was come up to Christian, he beheld him with a disdainful countenance, and thus began to question him.

APOLLYON: Whence came you, and whither are you bound?

CHRISTIAN: I am come from the city of Destruction, which is the place of all evil, and I

am going to the city of Zion.

APOLLYON: By this I perceive thou art one of my subjects; for all that country is mine, and I am the prince and god of it. How is it, then, that thou hast run away from thy king? Were it not that I hope thou mayest do me more service, I would strike thee now at one blow to the ground.

CHRISTIAN: I was, indeed, born in your dominions, but your service was hard, and your wages such as a man could not live on; for the wages of sin is death ; therefore, when I was come to years, I did, as other considerate persons do, look out if perhaps I might mend myself.

*Romans 6:23*

APOLLYON: There is no prince that will thus lightly lose his subjects, neither will I as yet lose thee; but since thou complainest of thy service and wages, be content to go back, and what our country will afford I do here promise to give thee.

CHRISTIAN: But I have let myself to another, even to the King of princes; and how can I with fairness go back with thee?

APOLLYON: Thou hast done in this according to the proverb, "changed a bad for a worse;" but it is ordinary for those that have professed themselves his servants, after a while to give him the slip, and return again to me. Do thou so to, and all shall be well.

CHRISTIAN: I have given him my faith, and sworn my allegiance to him; how then can I go back from this, and not be hanged as a traitor.

APOLLYON: Thou didst the same by me, and yet I am willing to pass by all, if now thou wilt yet turn again and go back.

CHRISTIAN: What I promised thee was in my non-age: and besides, I count that the Prince, under whose banner I now stand, is able to absolve me, yea, and to pardon also what I did as to my compliance with thee. And besides, O thou destroying Apollyon, to speak truth, I like his service, his wages, his servants, his government, his company, and country, better than thine; therefore leave off to persuade me farther: I am his servant, and I will follow him.

APOLLYON: Consider again, when thou art in cool blood, what thou art like to meet with in the way that thou goest. Thou knowest that for the most part his servants come to an ill end, because they are transgressors against me and my ways. How many of them have been put to shameful deaths! And besides, thou countest his service better than mine; whereas he never yet came from the place where he is, to deliver any that served him out of their enemies' hands: but as for me, how many times, as all the world very well knows, have I delivered, either by power or fraud, those that have faithfully served me, from him and his, though taken by them! And so will I deliver thee.

CHRISTIAN: His forbearing at present to deliver them, is on purpose to try their love, whether they will cleave to him to the end: and as for the ill end thou sayest they come to, that is most glorious in their account. For, for present deliverance, they do not much expect it; for they stay for their glory; and then they shall have it, when their Prince comes in his and the glory of the angels.

APOLLYON: Thou hast already been unfaithful in thy service to him; and how dost thou think to receive wages of him?

CHRISTIAN: Wherein, O Apollyon, have I been unfaithful to him?

APOLLYON: Thou didst faint at first setting out, when thou wast almost choked in the gulf of Despond. Thou didst attempt wrong ways to be rid of thy burden, whereas thou shouldst have stayed till thy Prince had taken it off. Thou didst sinfully sleep, and lose thy choice things. Thou wast almost persuaded also to go back at the sight of the lions. And when thou talkest of thy journey, and of what thou hast seen and heard, thou art inwardly desirous of vainglory in all that thou sayest or doest.

CHRISTIAN: All this is true, and much more which thou hast left out; but the Prince whom I serve and honor is merciful, and ready to forgive. But besides, these infirmities possessed me in thy country, for there I sucked them in, and I have groaned under them, been sorry for them, and have obtained pardon of my Prince.

APOLLYON: Then Apollyon broke out into a grievous rage, saying, I am an enemy to this Prince; I hate his person, his laws, and people: I am come out on purpose to withstand thee.

CHRISTIAN: Apollyon, beware what you do, for I am in the King's highway, the way of holiness; therefore take heed to yourself.

APOLLYON: Then Apollyon straddled quite over the whole breadth of the way, and said, I am void of fear in this matter. Prepare thyself to die; for I swear by my infernal den, that thou shalt go no farther: here will I spill thy soul. And with that he threw a flaming dart at his breast; but Christian had a shield in his hand, with which he caught it, and so prevented the danger of that.

Then did Christian draw, for he saw it was time to bestir him; and Apollyon as fast made at him, throwing darts as thick as hail; by the which, notwithstanding all that Christian could do to avoid it, Apollyon wounded him in his head, his hand, and foot. This made Christian give a little back: Apollyon, therefore, followed his work amain, and Christian again took courage, and resisted as manfully as he could. This sore combat lasted for above half a day, even till Christian was almost quite spent: for you must know, that Christian, by reason of his wounds, must needs grow weaker and weaker.

Then Apollyon, espying his opportunity, began to gather up close to Christian, and wrestling with him, gave him a dreadful fall; and with that Christian's sword flew out of his hand. Then said Apollyon, I am sure of thee now: and with that he had almost pressed him to death, so that Christian began to despair of life. But, as God would have it, while Apollyon was fetching his last blow, thereby to make a full end of this good man, Christian nimbly reached out his hand for his sword, and caught it, saying, Rejoice not against me, O mine *Micah 7:8* enemy: when I fall, I shall arise; and with that gave him a deadly thrust, which made him give back, as one that had received his mortal wound. Christian perceiving that, made at him again, saying, Nay, in all these things we are more than conquerors, through Him that loved *Romans 8:37* us. And with that Apollyon spread forth his dragon wings, and sped him away, that Christian for a season *James 4:7* saw him no more.

# 18

# EVIL REPORT, VALLEY OF SHADOW OF DEATH

I N THIS combat no man can imagine, unless he had seen and heard, as I did, what yelling and hideous roaring Apollyon made all the time of the fight; he spake like a dragon: and on the other side, what sighs and groans burst from Christian's heart. I never saw him all the while give so much as one pleasant look, till he perceived he had wounded Apollyon with his two-edged sword; then, indeed, he did smile, and look upward! But it was the dreadfullest sight that ever I saw.

> A more unequal match can hardly be
> Christian must fight an angel, But you see
> The valiant man by handling sword and shield
> Make him the dragon quit the field.

So when the battle was over, Christian said, I will here give thanks to him that hath delivered me out of the mouth of the lion, to him that did help me against Apollyon. And so he did, saying,

> "Great Beelzebub, the captain of this fiend,
> Designed my ruin; therefore to this end
> He sent him harness'd out; and he, with rage
> That hellish was, did fiercely me engage:
> But blessed Michael helped me, and I,
> By dint of sword, did quickly make him fly:
> Therefore to Him let me give lasting praise,

And thank and bless his holy name always."

Then there came to him a hand with some of the leaves of the tree of life, the which Christian took and applied to the wounds that he had received in the battle, and was healed immediately. He also sat down in that place to eat bread, and to drink of the bottle that was given him a little before: so, being refreshed, he addressed himself to his journey with his sword drawn in his hand; for he said, I know not but some other enemy may be at hand. But he met with no other affront from Apollyon quite through this valley.

Now at the end of this valley was another, called the Valley of the Shadow of Death; and Christian must needs go through it, because the way to the Celestial City lay through the midst of it. Now, this valley is a very solitary place. The prophet Jeremiah thus describes it: "A wilderness, a land of deserts and pits, a land of drought, and of the Shadow of Death, a land that no man" (but a Christian) *Jeremiah 2:6* "passeth through, and where no man dwelt."

Now here Christian was worse put to it than in his fight with Apollyon, as by the sequel you shall see.

I saw then in my dream, that when Christian was got to the borders of the Shadow of Death, there met him two men, children of them that brought up an evil *Numbers 13:32* report of the good land, making haste to go back; to whom Christian spake as follows.

CHRISTIAN: Whither are you going?

THE TWO MEN: They said, Back, back; and we would have you do so too, if either life or peace is prized by you.

CHRISTIAN: Why, what's the matter? said Christian.

THE TWO MEN: Matter! said they; we were

going that way as you are going, and went as far as we durst: and indeed we were almost past coming back; for had we gone a little further, we had not been here to bring the news to thee.

CHRISTIAN: But what have you met with? said Christian.

THE TWO MEN: Why, we were almost in the Valley of the Shadow of Death, but that by good

Psalm 44:19;
107:19

hap we looked before us, and saw the danger be-fore we came to it.

CHRISTIAN: But what have you seen? said Christian.

THE TWO MEN: Seen! why the valley itself, which is as dark as pitch: we also saw there the hobgoblins, satyrs, and dragons of the pit: we heard also in that valley a continual howling and yelling, as of a people under unutterable misery, who there sat bound in affliction and irons: and over that valley hang the discouraging clouds of confusion: Death also doth always spread his wings over it. In a word, it is every whit dreadful, being utterly without order.

Job 3:5; 10:22

CHRISTIAN: Then, said Christian, I perceive not yet, by what you have said, but that this is my way to the desired haven.

Psalm 44:18–19
Jeremiah 2:6

THE TWO MEN: Be it thy way; we will not choose it for ours.

So they parted, and Christian went on his way, but still with his sword drawn in his hand, for fear lest he should be assaulted.

I saw then in my dream, so far as this valley reached, there was on the right hand a very deep ditch; that ditch is it into which the blind have led the blind in all ages, and have both there miserably perished. Again, behold, on the left hand there was a very dangerous quag, into which, if even a good man falls, he finds no bottom for his foot to stand on: into that quag king David once did fall, and had no doubt therein been smothered, had not He that is able plucked him out.

Psalm 69:14

The pathway was here also exceeding narrow, and therefore good Christian was the more put to it; for when he sought, in the dark, to shun the ditch on the one hand, he was ready to tip over into the mire on the other; also, when he sought to escape the mire, without great carefulness he would be ready to fall into the ditch. Thus he went on, and I heard him here sigh bitterly; for besides the danger mentioned above, the pathway was here so dark, that ofttimes when he lifted up his foot to go forward, he knew not where, or upon what he should set it next.

> Poor man, where art thou now? Thy day is night
> Good man, Be not cast down, Thou yet art right
> Thy way to heaven lies by the gate of hell
> Cheer up, hold out, With thee it shall go well.

About the midst of this valley I perceived the mouth of hell to be, and it stood also hard by the wayside. Now, thought Christian, what shall I do? And ever and anon the flame and smoke would come out in such abundance, with sparks and hideous noises, (things that cared not for Christian's sword, as did Apollyon before,) that he was forced to put up his sword, and betake himself to another weapon, called All-prayer; so he cried, in my hearing, O Lord, I beseech thee, deliver my soul. Thus he went on a great while, yet still the flames would be reaching towards him; also he heard doleful voices, and rushings to and fro, so that sometimes he thought he should be torn in pieces, or trodden down like mire in the streets. This frightful sight was seen, and these dreadful noises were heard by him for several miles together; and coming to a place where he thought he heard a company of fiends coming forward to meet him, he stopped, and began to muse what he had best to do. Sometimes he had half a thought to go back; then again he thought he might be half-way through the valley. He remembered also, how he had already vanquished many a danger; and that the danger of going back might be much more than for to go forward. So he resolved to go on; yet the fiends seemed to come nearer and nearer. But when

*Ephesians 6:18*

*Psalm 116:4*

they were come even almost at him, he cried out with a most vehement voice, I will walk in the strength of the Lord God. So they gave back, and came no farther.

One thing I would not let slip. I took notice that now poor Christian was so confounded that he did not know his own voice; and thus I perceived it. Just when he was come over against the mouth of the burning pit, one of the wicked ones got behind him, and stepped up softly to him, and whisperingly suggested many grievous blasphemies to him, which he verily thought had proceeded from his own mind. This put Christian more to it than any thing that he met with before, even to think that he should now blaspheme Him that he loved so much before. Yet if he could have helped it, he would not have done it; but he had not the discretion either to stop his ears, or to know from whence these blasphemies came.

When Christian had travelled in this disconsolate condition some considerable time, he thought he heard the voice of a man, as going before him, saying, Though I walk through the Valley of the Shadow of Death, I will *Psalm 23:4* fear no evil, for thou art with me.

Then was he glad, and that for these reasons:

First, Because he gathered from thence, that some who feared God were in this valley as well as himself.

Secondly, For that he perceived God was with them, though in that dark and dismal state. And why not, thought he, with me? though by reason of the impedi-*Job 9:11* ment that attends this place, I cannot perceive it.

Thirdly, For that he hoped (could he overtake them) to have company by and by.

So he went on, and called to him that was before; but he knew not what to answer, for that he also thought himself to be alone. And by and by the day broke: then said Christian, "He hath turned the shadow of death *Amos 5:8* into the morning."

Now morning being come, he looked back, not out of desire to return, but to see, by the light of the day, what hazards he had gone through in the dark. So he saw more perfectly the ditch that was on the one hand, and the quag that was on the other; also how narrow the way was which led betwixt them both. Also now he saw the hobgoblins, and satyrs, and dragons of the pit, but all afar off; for after break of day they came not nigh; yet they were discovered to him, according to that which is written, "He discovereth deep things out of darkness, and bringeth out to light the shadow of death."

*Job 12:22*

Now was Christian much affected with this deliverance from all the dangers of his solitary way; which dangers, though he feared them much before, yet he saw them more clearly now, because the light of the day made them conspicuous to him. And about this time the sun was rising, and this was another mercy to Christian; for you must note, that though the first part of the Valley of the Shadow of Death was dangerous, yet this second part, which he was yet to go, was, if possible, far more dangerous; for, from the place where he now stood, even to the end of the valley, the way was all along set so full of snares, traps, gins, and nets here, and so full of pits, pitfalls, deep holes, and shelvings-down there, that had it now been dark, as it was when he came the first part of the way, had he had a thousand souls, they had in reason been cast away; but, as I said, just now the sun was rising. Then said he, "His Candle shineth on my head, and by his light I go through darkness."

*Job 29:3*

In this light, therefore, he came to the end of the valley. Now I saw in my dream, that at the end of the valley lay blood, bones, ashes, and mangled bodies of men, even of pilgrims that had gone this way formerly; and while I was musing what should be the reason, I espied a little before me a cave, where two giants, Pope and Pagan, dwelt in old times; by whose power and tyranny the men whose bones, blood, ashes, etc., lay there, were cruelly put to death. But by this place Christian went without much danger, whereat I somewhat wondered; but I have learnt since, that Pagan has been dead many a day; and as for the other, though he be yet alive, he is, by reason of age, and also of the many shrewd brushes that he met with in his younger days, grown so crazy and stiff in his joints that he can now do little more than sit in his cave's mouth, grinning at pilgrims as they go by, and biting his nails because he cannot come at them.

So I saw that Christian went on his way; yet, at the sight of the old man that sat at the mouth of the cave, he could not tell what to think, especially because he spoke to him, though he could not go after him, saying, You will never mend, till more of you be burned. But he held his peace, and set a good face on it; and so went by, and catched no hurt.

Then sang Christian,

"O world of wonders, (I can say no less,)
That I should be preserved in that distress
That I have met with here! O blessed be
That hand that from it hath delivered me!
Dangers in darkness, devils, hell, and sin,
Did compass me, while I this vale was in;
Yea, snares, and pits, and traps, and nets did lie
My path about, that worthless, silly I
Might have been catch'd, entangled, and cast down;
But since I live, let Jesus wear the crown."

# 19

# FAITHFUL, ADAM
# & MOSES

NOW, AS Christian went on his way, he came to a little ascent, which was cast up on purpose that pilgrims might see before them: up there, therefore, Christian went; and looking forward, he saw Faithful before him upon his journey: Then said Christian aloud, Ho, ho; so-ho; stay, and I will be your companion. At that Faithful looked behind him; to whom Christian cried again, Stay, stay, till I come up to you. But Faithful answered, No, I am upon my life, and the avenger of blood is behind me.

At this Christian was somewhat moved, and putting to all his strength, he quickly got up with Faithful, and did also overrun him; so the last was first. Then did Christian vaingloriously smile, because he had gotten the start of his brother; but not taking good heed to his feet, he suddenly stumbled and fell, and could not rise again until Faithful came up to help him.

Then I saw in my dream, they went very lovingly on together, and had sweet discourse of all things that had happened to them in their pilgrimage; and thus Christian began.

CHRISTIAN: My honored and well-beloved brother Faithful, I am glad that I have overtaken you, and that God has so tempered our spirits that we can walk as companions in this so pleasant a path.

FAITHFUL: I had thought, my dear friend, to have had your company quite from our town, but you did get the start of me; wherefore I was forced to come thus much of the way alone.

CHRISTIAN: How long did you stay in the city of Destruction before you set out after me on your pilgrimage?

FAITHFUL: Till I could stay no longer; for there was a great talk presently after you were gone out, that our city would, in a short time, with fire from heaven, be burnt down to the ground.

CHRISTIAN: What, did your neighbors talk so?

FAITHFUL: Yes, it was for a while in every body's mouth.

CHRISTIAN: What, and did no more of them but you come out to escape the danger?

FAITHFUL: Though there was, as I said, a great talk thereabout, yet I do not think they did firmly believe it; for, in the heat of the discourse, I heard some of them deridingly speak of you and of your desperate journey, for so they called this your pilgrimage. But I did believe, and do still, that the end of our city will be with fire and brimstone from above; and therefore I have made my escape.

CHRISTIAN: Did you hear no talk of neighbor Pliable?

FAITHFUL: Yes, Christian, I heard that he followed you till he came to the Slough of Despond, where, as some said, he fell in; but he would not be known to have so done: but I am sure he was soundly bedabbled with that kind of dirt.

CHRISTIAN: And what said the neighbors to him?

FAITHFUL: He hath, since his going back, been had greatly in derision, and that among all sorts of people: some do mock and despise him, and scarce will any set him on work. He is now seven times worse than if he had never gone out of the city.

CHRISTIAN: But why should they be so set against him, since they also despise the way that he forsook?

FAITHFUL: O, they say, Hang him; he is a turncoat; he was not true to his profession! I think God has stirred up even His enemies to hiss at him, and make him a proverb, because he hath forsaken the way.

*Jeremiah 29:18–19*

CHRISTIAN: Had you no talk with him before you came out?

FAITHFUL: I met him once in the streets, but he leered away on the other side, as one ashamed of what he had done; So I spake not to him.

CHRISTIAN: Well, at my first setting out I had hopes of that man; but now I fear he will perish in the overthrow of the city. For it has happened to him according to the true proverb, The dog is turned to his vomit again, and the sow that was washed to her wallowing in the mire.

*2 Peter 2:22*

FAITHFUL: These are my fears of him too; but who can hinder that which will be?

CHRISTIAN: Well, neighbor Faithful, said Christian, let us leave him, and talk of things that more immediately concern ourselves. Tell me now what you have met with in the way as you came; for I know you have met with some things, or else it may be writ for a wonder.

FAITHFUL: I escaped the slough that I perceive you fell into, and got up to the gate without that danger; only I met with one whose name was Wanton, that had like to have done me mischief.

CHRISTIAN: It was well you escaped her net: Joseph was hard put to it by her, and he escaped her as you did; but it had like to have cost him *Genesis 39:11–13* his life. But what did she do to you?

FAITHFUL: You cannot think (but that you know something) what a flattering tongue she had; she lay at me hard to turn aside with her, promising me all manner of content.

CHRISTIAN: Nay, she did not promise you the content of a good conscience.

FAITHFUL: You know what I mean; all carnal and fleshly content.

CHRISTIAN: Thank God that you escaped her: *Proverbs 22:14* the abhorred of the Lord shall fall into her pit.

FAITHFUL: Nay, I know not whether I did wholly escape her or no.

CHRISTIAN: Why, I trow you did not consent to her desires?

FAITHFUL: No, not to defile myself; for I re- membered an old writing that I had seen, which *Proverbs 5:5* said, "Her steps take hold on Hell."

So I shut mine eyes, because I would not be be-
witched with her looks. Then she railed on me,
and I went my way.

Job 31:1

CHRISTIAN: Did you meet with no other assault as you came?

FAITHFUL: When I came to the foot of the hill
called Difficulty, I met with a very aged man, who
asked me what I was, and whither bound. I told

him that I was a pilgrim, going to the Celestial City. Then said the old man, Thou lookest like an honest fellow; wilt thou be content to dwell with me for the wages that I shall give thee? Then I asked his name, and where he dwelt? He said his name was Adam the First, and that he dwelt in the town of Deceit. I asked him then what was his work, and what the wages that he would give. He told me that his work was *many delights*; and his wages, that I should be his heir at last. I further asked him, what house he kept, and what other servants he had. So he told me that his house was maintained with all the dainties of the world, and that his servants were those of his own begetting. Then I asked how many children he had. He said that he had but three daughters, the Lust of the Flesh, the Lust of the Eyes, and the Pride of Life, and that I should marry them if I would. Then I asked, how long time he would have me live with him; And he told me, as long as he lived himself.

*Ephesians 4:22*

*1 John 2:16*

CHRISTIAN: Well, and what conclusion came the old man and you to at last?

FAITHFUL: Why, at first I found myself somewhat inclinable to go with the man, for I thought he spake very fair; but looking in his forehead, as I talked with him, I saw there written, "Put off the old man with his deeds."

CHRISTIAN: And how then?

FAITHFUL: Then it came burning hot into my mind, that, whatever he said, and however he flattered, when he got me home to his house he would sell me for a slave. So I bid him forbear to talk, for I would not come near the door of his house. Then he reviled me, and told me that he would send such a one after me that should make my way bitter to my soul. So I turned to go away from him; but just as I turned myself to go thence, I felt him take hold of my flesh, and give me such a deadly twitch back, that I thought he had pulled part of me after himself: this made me cry, "O wretched man." So I went on my way up the hill.

*Romans 7:24*

Now, when I had got above half-way up, I looked behind me, and saw one coming after me, swift as the wind; so he overtook me just about the place where the settle stands.

CHRISTIAN: Just there, said Christian, did I sit down to rest me; but being overcome with sleep, I there lost this roll out of my bosom.

FAITHFUL: But, good brother, hear me out. So soon as the man overtook me, it was but a word and a blow; for down he knocked me, and laid me for dead. But when I was a little come to myself again I asked him wherefore he served me so. He said because of my secret inclining to Adam the First. And with that he struck me another deadly blow on the breast, and beat me down backward; so I lay at his foot as dead as before. So when I came to myself again I cried him mercy: but he said, I know not how to show mercy; and with that he knocked me down again. He had doubtless made an end of me, but that one came by and bid him forbear.

CHRISTIAN: Who was that that bid him forbear?

FAITHFUL: I did not know him at first: but as

he went by, I perceived the holes in his hands and in his side: Then I concluded that he was our Lord. So I went up the hill.

CHRISTIAN: That man that overtook you was Moses. He spareth none; neither knoweth he how to shew mercy to those that transgress the law.

FAITHFUL: I know it very well; it was not the first time that he has met with me. 'Twas he that came to me when I dwelt securely at home, and that told me he would burn my house over my head if I stayed there.

CHRISTIAN: But did you not see the house that stood there on the top of the hill, on the side of which Moses met you?

FAITHFUL: Yes, and the lions too, before I came at it. But, for the lions, I think they were asleep, for it was about noon; and because I had so much of the day before me, I passed by the Porter, and came down the hill.

CHRISTIAN: He told me, indeed, that he saw you go by; but I wish you had called at the house, for they would have showed you so many rarities that you would scarce have forgot them to the day of your death. But pray tell me, Did you meet nobody in the Valley of Humility?

# 20

# DISCONTENT & SHAME

FAITHFUL: YES, I met with one Discontent, who would willingly have persuaded me to go back again with him: his reason was, for that the valley was altogether without honor. He told me, moreover, that to go there was the way to disoblige all my friends, as Pride, Arrogancy, Self-Conceit, Worldly Glory, with others, who he knew, as he said, would be very much offended if I made such a fool of myself as to wade through this valley.

CHRISTIAN: Well, and how did you answer him?

FAITHFUL: I told him, that although all these that he named, might claim a kindred of me, and that rightly, (for indeed they were my relations according to the flesh,) yet since I became a pilgrim they have disowned me, and I also have rejected them; and therefore they were to me now no more than if they had never been of my lineage. I told him, moreover, that as to this valley, he had quite misrepresented the thing; for before honor is humility, and a haughty spirit before a fall. Therefore, said I, I had rather go through this valley to the honor that was so accounted by the wisest, than choose that which he esteemed most worthy of our affections.

CHRISTIAN: Met you with nothing else in that valley?

FAITHFUL: Yes, I met with Shame; but of all the men that I met with on my pilgrimage, he, I think, bears the wrong name. The other would be said nay, after a little argumentation, and somewhat else; but this bold-faced Shame would never have done.

CHRISTIAN: Why, what did he say to you?

FAITHFUL: What? why, he objected against religion itself. He said it was a pitiful, low, sneaking business for a man to mind religion. He said, that a tender conscience was an unmanly thing; and that for a man to watch over his words and ways, so as to tie up himself from that hectoring liberty that the brave spirits of the times accustomed themselves unto, would make him the ridicule of the times. He objected also, that but few of the mighty, rich, or wise, were ever of my opinion; nor any of them neither, before they were persuaded to be fools, and to be of a voluntary fondness to venture the loss of all for nobody knows what. He, moreover, objected the base and low estate and condition of those that were chiefly the pilgrims of the times in which they lived; also their ignorance and want of understanding in all natural science. Yea, he did hold me to it at that rate also, about a great many more things than here I relate; as, that it was a shame to sit whining and mourning under a sermon, and a shame to come sighing and groaning home; that it was a shame to ask my neighbor forgiveness for petty faults, or to make restitution where I have taken from any. He said also, that religion made a man grow strange to the great, because of a few vices, which he called by finer names, and made him own and respect

*1 Corinthians 1:26;*
*3:18*
*Philippians 3:7–9*
*John 7:48*

the base, because of the same religious fraternity: And is not this, said he, a shame?

CHRISTIAN: And what did you say to him?

FAITHFUL: Say? I could not tell what to say at first. Yea, he put me so to it, that my blood came up in my face; even this Shame fetched it up, and had almost beat me quite off. But at last I began to consider, that that which is highly esteemed among men, is had in abomination with God. And I thought again, this Shame tells me what men are; but he tells me nothing what God, or the word of God is. And I thought, moreover, that at the day of doom we shall not be doomed to death or life according to the hectoring spirits of the world, but according to the wisdom and law of the Highest. Therefore, thought I, what God says is best, is indeed best, though all the men in the world are against it. Seeing, then, that God prefers his religion; seeing God prefers a tender Conscience; seeing they that make themselves fools for the kingdom of heaven are wisest, and that the poor man that loveth Christ is richer than the greatest man in the world that hates him; Shame, depart, thou art an enemy to my salvation. Shall I entertain thee against my sovereign Lord? How then shall I look him in the face at his coming? Should I now be ashamed of his ways and servants, how can I expect the blessing? But indeed this Shame was a bold villain; I could scarcely shake him out of my company; yea, he would be haunting of me, and continually whispering me in the ear, with some one or other of the infirmities that attend religion. But at last I told him, that it was but in vain to attempt farther in this

*Luke 16:15*

*Mark 8:38*

business; for those things that he disdained, in those did I see most glory: and so at last I got past this importunate one. And when I had shaken him off, then I began to sing,

"The trials that those men do meet withal,
That are obedient to the heavenly call,
Are manifold, and suited to the flesh,
And come, and come, and come again afresh;
That now, or some time else, we by them may
Be taken, overcome, and cast away.
O let the pilgrims, let the pilgrims then,
Be vigilant, and quit themselves like men."

CHRISTIAN: I am glad, my brother, that thou didst withstand this villain so bravely; for of all, as thou sayest, I think he has the wrong name; for he is so bold as to follow us in the streets, and to attempt to put us to shame before all men; that is, to make us ashamed of that which is good. But if he was not himself audacious, he would never attempt to do as he does. But let us still resist him; for, notwithstanding all his bravadoes, he promoteth the fool, and none else. "The wise shall inherit glory," said Solomon; "but shame shall be the promotion of fools."

*Proverbs 3:35*

FAITHFUL: I think we must cry to Him for help against Shame, that would have us to be valiant for truth upon the earth.

CHRISTIAN: You say true; but did you meet nobody else in that valley?

FAITHFUL: No, not I; for I had sunshine all the rest of the way through that, and also through the Valley of the Shadow of Death.

CHRISTIAN: 'Twas well for you; I am sure it

fared far otherwise with me. I had for a long season, as soon almost as I entered into that valley, a dreadful combat with that foul fiend Apollyon; yea, I thought verily he would have killed me, especially when he got me down, and crushed me under him, as if he would have crushed me to pieces; for as he threw me, my sword flew out of my hand: nay, he told me he was sure of me; but I cried to God, and he heard me, and delivered me out of all my troubles. Then I entered into the Valley of the Shadow of Death, and had no light for almost half the way through it. I thought I should have been killed there over and over; but at last day brake, and the sun rose, and I went through that which was behind with far more ease and quiet.

# 21

# TALKATIVE, CHRISTIAN
# & FAITHFUL

MOREOVER, I saw in my dream, that as they went on, Faithful, as he chanced to look on one side, saw a man whose name was Talkative, walking at a distance beside them; for in this place there was room enough for them all to walk. He was a tall man, and something more comely at a distance than at hand. To this man Faithful addressed himself in this manner.

FAITHFUL: Friend, whither away? Are you going to the heavenly country?

TALKATIVE: I am going to the same place.

FAITHFUL: That is well; then I hope we shall have your good company?

TALKATIVE: With a very good will, will I be your companion.

FAITHFUL: Come on, then, and let us go together, and let us spend our time in discoursing of things that are profitable.

TALKATIVE: To talk of things that are good, to me is very acceptable, with you or with any other; and I am glad that I have met with those that incline to so good a work; for, to speak the truth, there are but few who care thus to spend

their time as they are in their travels, but choose much rather to be speaking of things to no profit; and this hath been a trouble to me.

FAITHFUL: That is, indeed, a thing to be lamented; for what thing so worthy of the use of the tongue and mouth of men on earth, as are the things of the God of heaven?

TALKATIVE: I like you wonderful well, for your

saying is full of conviction; and I will add, What thing is so pleasant, and what so profitable, as to talk of the things of God? What things so pleasant? that is, if a man hath any delight in things that are wonderful. For instance, if a man doth delight to talk of the history, or the mystery of things; or if a man doth love to talk of miracles, wonders, or signs, where shall he find things recorded so delightful, and so sweetly penned, as in the holy Scripture?

FAITHFUL: That is true; but to be profited by such things in our talk, should be our chief design.

TALKATIVE: That's it that I said; for to talk of such things is most profitable; for by so doing a man may get knowledge of many things; as of the vanity of earthly things, and the benefit of things above. Thus in general; but more particularly, by this a man may learn the necessity of the new birth, the insufficiency of our works, the need of Christ's righteousness, etc. Besides, by this a man may learn what it is to repent, to believe, to pray, to suffer, or the like: by this, also, a man may learn what are the great promises and consolations of the Gospel, to his own comfort. Farther, by this a man may learn to refute false opinions, to vindicate the truth, and also to instruct the ignorant.

FAITHFUL: All this is true; and glad am I to hear these things from you.

TALKATIVE: Alas! the want of this is the cause that so few understand the need of faith, and the necessity of a work of grace in their soul, in order to eternal life; but ignorantly live in the works of the law, by which a man can by no means obtain the kingdom of heaven.

FAITHFUL: But, by your leave, heavenly knowledge of these is the gift of God; no man attaineth to them by human industry, or only by the talk of them.

TALKATIVE: All this I know very well; for a man can receive nothing, except it be given him from heaven: all is of grace, not of works. I could give you a hundred scriptures for the confirmation of this.

FAITHFUL: Well, then, said Faithful, what is that one thing that we shall at this time found our discourse upon?

TALKATIVE: What you will. I will talk of things heavenly, or things earthly; things moral, or things evangelical; things sacred, or things profane; things past, or things to come; things foreign, or things at home; things more essential, or things circumstantial: provided that all be done to our profit.

FAITHFUL: Now did Faithful begin to wonder; and stepping to Christian, (for he walked all this while by himself,) he said to him, but softly, What a brave companion have we got! Surely, this man will make a very excellent pilgrim.

CHRISTIAN: At this Christian modestly smiled, and said, This man, with whom you are so taken, will beguile with this tongue of his, twenty of them that know him not.

FAITHFUL: Do you know him, then?

CHRISTIAN: Know him? Yes, better than he

knows himself.

FAITHFUL: Pray what is he?

CHRISTIAN: His name is Talkative: he dwelleth in our town. I wonder that you should be a stranger to him, only I consider that our town is large.

FAITHFUL: Whose son is he? And whereabout doth he dwell?

CHRISTIAN: He is the son of one Say-well. He dwelt in Prating-Row; and he is known to all that are acquainted with him by the name of Talkative of Prating-Row; and, notwithstanding his fine tongue, he is but a sorry fellow.

FAITHFUL: Well, he seems to be a very pretty man.

CHRISTIAN: That is, to them that have not a thorough acquaintance with him, for he is best abroad; near home he is ugly enough. Your saying that he is a pretty man, brings to my mind what I have observed in the work of a painter, whose pictures show best at a distance; but very near, more unpleasing.

FAITHFUL: But I am ready to think you do but jest, because you smiled.

CHRISTIAN: God forbid that I should jest (though I smiled) in this matter, or that I should accuse any falsely. I will give you a further discovery of him. This man is for any company, and for any talk; as he talketh now with you, so will he talk when he is on the ale-bench; and the more drink he hath in his crown, the more of these things he hath in his mouth. Religion hath no place in his heart, or house, or conversation; all he hath lieth in his tongue, and his religion is to make a noise therewith.

FAITHFUL: Say you so? Then am I in this man greatly deceived.

CHRISTIAN: Deceived! you may be sure of it. Remember the proverb, "They say, and do not;" but the kingdom of God is not in word, but in power. He talketh of prayer, of repentance, of faith, and of the new birth; but he knows but only to talk of them. I have been in his family, and have observed him both at home and abroad; and I know what I say of him is the truth. His house is as empty of religion as the white of an egg is of savor. There is there neither prayer, nor sign of repentance for sin; yea, the brute, in his kind, serves God far better than he. He is the very stain, reproach, and shame of religion to all that know him; it can hardly have a good word in all that end of the town where he dwells, through him. Thus say the common people that know him, "A saint abroad, and a devil at home." His poor family finds it so; he is such a churl, such a railer at, and so unreasonable with his servants, that they neither know how to do for or speak to him. Men that have any dealings with him say, It is better to deal with a Turk than with him, for fairer dealings they shall have at their hands. This Talkative (if it be possible) will go beyond them, defraud, beguile, and overreach them. Besides, he brings up his sons to follow his steps; and if he finds in any of them a foolish timorousness, (for so he calls the first appearance of a tender conscience,) he calls them fools and blockheads, and by no means will employ them in much, or speak to their com-

*Matthew 23:3*
*1 Corinthians 4:20*

*Romans 2:24–25*

mendation before others. For my part, I am of opinion that he has, by his wicked life, caused many to stumble and fall; and will be, if God prevents not, the ruin of many more.

FAITHFUL: Well, my brother, I am bound to believe you, not only because you say you know him, but also because, like a Christian, you make your reports of men. For I cannot think that you speak these things of ill-will, but because it is even so as you say.

CHRISTIAN: Had I known him no more than you, I might, perhaps, have thought of him as at the first you did; yea, had I received this report at their hands only that are enemies to religion, I should have thought it had been a slander—a lot that often falls from bad men's mouths upon good men's names and professions. But all these things, yea, and a great many more as bad, of my own knowledge, I can prove him guilty of. Besides, good men are ashamed of him; they can neither call him brother nor friend; the very naming of him among them makes them blush, if they know him.

FAITHFUL: Well, I see that saying and doing are two things, and hereafter I shall better observe this distinction.

CHRISTIAN: They are two things indeed, and are as diverse as are the soul and the body; for, as the body without the soul is but a dead carcass, so saying, if it be alone, is but a dead carcass also. The soul of religion is the practical part. "Pure religion and undefiled before God and the Father is this, to visit the fatherless and widows in their affliction, and to keep himself unspotted from

James 1:27
(see also verses
22–26)

the world." This, Talkative is not aware of; he thinks that hearing and saying will make a good Christian; and thus he deceiveth his own soul. Hearing is but as the sowing of the seed; talking is not sufficient to prove that fruit is indeed in the heart and life. And let us assure ourselves, that at the day of doom men shall be judged according to their fruits. It will not be said then, Did you believe? but, Were you doers, or talkers only? and accordingly shall they be judged. The end of the world is compared to our harvest, and you know men at harvest regard nothing but fruit. Not that any thing can be accepted that is not of faith; but I speak this to show you how insignificant the profession of Talkative will be at that day.

Matthew 13:23

Matthew 13:30

FAITHFUL: This brings to my mind that of Moses, by which he describeth the beast that is clean. He is such an one that parteth the hoof, and cheweth the cud; not that parteth the hoof only, or that cheweth the cud only. The hare cheweth the cud, but yet is unclean, because he parteth not the hoof. And this truly resembleth Talkative: he cheweth the cud, he seeketh knowledge; he cheweth upon the word, but he divideth not the hoof. He parteth not with the way of sinners; but, as the hare, he retaineth the foot of the dog or bear, and therefore he is unclean.

Leviticus 11
Deuteronomy 14

CHRISTIAN: You have spoken, for aught I know, the true gospel sense of these texts. And I will add another thing: Paul calleth some men, yea, and those great talkers too, sounding brass, and tinkling cymbals ; that is, as he expounds them in another place, things without life giving sound. Things without life; that is, without the

1 Corinthians 13:1, 3

1 Corinthians 14:7

true faith and grace of the gospel; and consequently, things that shall never be placed in the kingdom of heaven among those that are the children of life; though their sound, by their talk, be as if it were the tongue or voice of an angel.

FAITHFUL: Well, I was not so fond of his company at first, but I am as sick of it now. What shall we do to be rid of him?

CHRISTIAN: Take my advice, and do as I bid you, and you shall find that he will soon be sick of your company too, except God shall touch his heart, and turn it.

FAITHFUL: What would you have me to do?

CHRISTIAN: Why, go to him, and enter into some serious discourse about the power of religion; and ask him plainly, (when he has approved of it, for that he will,) whether this thing be set up in his heart, house, or conversation.

# 22

# FAITHFUL & TALKATIVE

FAITHFUL: THEN Faithful stepped forward again, and said to Talkative, Come, what cheer? How is it now?

TALKATIVE: Thank you, well: I thought we should have had a great deal of talk by this time.

FAITHFUL: Well, if you will, we will fall to it now; and since you left it with me to state the question, let it be this: How doth the saving grace of God discover itself when it is in the heart of man?

TALKATIVE: I perceive, then, that our talk must be about the power of things. Well, it is a very good question, and I shall be willing to answer you. And take my answer in brief, thus: First, where the grace of God is in the heart, it causeth there a great outcry against sin. Secondly-

FAITHFUL: Nay, hold; let us consider of one at once. I think you should rather say, it shows itself by inclining the soul to abhor its sin.

TALKATIVE: Why, what difference is there between crying out against, and abhorring of sin?

FAITHFUL: Oh! a great deal. A man may cry

out against sin, of policy; but he cannot abhor it but by virtue of a godly antipathy against it. I have heard many cry out against sin in the pulpit, who yet can abide it well enough in the heart, house, and conversation. Joseph's mistress cried out with a loud voice, as if she had been very holy; but she would willingly, notwithstanding that, have committed uncleanness with him. Some cry out against sin, even as the mother cries out against her child in her lap, when she calleth it slut and naughty girl, and then falls to hugging and kissing it.

*Genesis 39:15*

TALKATIVE: You lie at the catch, I perceive.

FAITHFUL: No, not I; I am only for setting things right. But what is the second thing whereby you would prove a discovery of a work of grace in the heart?

TALKATIVE: Great knowledge of gospel mysteries.

FAITHFUL: This sign should have been first: but, first or last, it is also false; for knowledge, great knowledge, may be obtained in the mysteries of the Gospel, and yet no work of grace in the soul. Yea, if a man have all knowledge, he may yet be nothing, and so, consequently, be no child of God. When Christ said, "Do you know all these things?" and the disciples answered, Yes, he added, "Blessed are ye if ye do them." He doth not lay the blessing in the knowing of them, but in the doing of them. For there is a knowledge that is not attended with doing: "He that knoweth his Master's will, and doeth it not." A man may know like an angel, and yet be no Christian: therefore your sign of it is not true.

*1 Corinthians 13:2*

Indeed, to *know* is a thing that pleaseth talkers and boasters; but to *do* is that which pleaseth God. Not that the heart can be good without knowledge, for without that the heart is naught. There are, therefore, two sorts of knowledge, knowledge that resteth in the bare speculation of things, and knowledge that is accompanied with the grace of faith and love, which puts a man upon doing even the will of God from the heart: the first of these will serve the talker; but without the other, the true Christian is not content. "Give me understanding, and I shall keep thy law; yea, I shall observe it with my whole heart."

*Psalm 119:34*

TALKATIVE: You lie at the catch again: this is not for edification.

FAITHFUL: Well, if you please, propound another sign how this work of grace discovereth itself where it is.

TALKATIVE: Not I, for I see we shall not agree.

FAITHFUL: Well, if you will not, will you give me leave to do it?

TALKATIVE: You may use your liberty.

FAITHFUL: A work of grace in the soul discovereth itself, either to him that hath it, or to standers-by.

To him that hath it, thus: It gives him conviction of sin, especially the defilement of his nature, and the sin of unbelief, for the sake of which he is sure to be damned, if he findeth not mercy at God's hand, by faith in Jesus Christ.

Psalm 38:18
Jeremiah 31:19
John 16:8
Romans 7:24
Mark 16:16
Galatians 2:16
Revelation 1:6

This sight and sense of things worketh in him sorrow and shame for sin. He findeth, moreover, revealed in him the Saviour of the world, and the absolute necessity of closing with him for life; at the which he findeth hungerings and thirstings after him; to which hungerings, etc., the promise is made. Now, according to the strength or weakness of his faith in his Saviour, so is his joy and peace, so is his love to holiness, so are his desires to know him more, and also to serve him in this world. But though, I say, it discovereth itself thus unto him, yet it is but seldom that he is able to conclude that this is a work of grace; because his corruptions now, and his abused reason, make his mind to misjudge in this matter: therefore in him that hath this work there is required a very sound judgment, before he can with steadiness conclude that this is a work of grace.

John 16:9
Galatians 2:15–16
Acts 4:12
Matthew 5:6
Revelation 21:6

To others it is thus discovered:

1. By an experimental confession of his faith in Christ.

2. By a life answerable to that confession; to wit, a life of holiness-heart-holiness, family-holiness, (if he hath a family,) and by conversation-holiness in the world; which in the general teacheth him inwardly to abhor his sin, and himself for that, in secret; to suppress it in his family, and to promote holiness in the world: not by talk only, as a hypocrite or talkative person may do, but by a practical subjection in faith and love to the power of the word. And now, sir, as to this brief description of the work of grace,

Job 42:5–6
Psalm 50:23
Ezekiel 20:43
Matthew 5:8
John 14:15
Romans 10:10
Ezekiel 36:25
Philippians 1:27;
3:17–20

and also the discovery of it, if you have aught to object, object; if not, then give me leave to propound to you a second question.

TALKATIVE: Nay, my part is not now to object, but to hear; let me, therefore, have your second question.

FAITHFUL: It is this: Do you experience this first part of the description of it; and doth your life and conversation testify the same? Or standeth your religion in word or tongue, and not in deed and truth? Pray, if you incline to answer me in this, say no more than you know the God above will say Amen to, and also nothing but what your conscience can justify you in; for not he that commendeth himself is approved, but whom the Lord commendeth. Besides, to say I am thus and thus, when my conversation, and all my neighbors, tell me I lie, is great wickedness.

Then Talkative at first began to blush; but, recovering himself, thus he replied: You come now to experience, to conscience, and to God; and to appeal to him for justification of what is spoken. This kind of discourse I did not expect; nor am I disposed to give an answer to such questions, because I count not myself bound thereto, unless you take upon you to be a catechiser; and though you should so do, yet I may refuse to make you my judge. But I pray, will you tell me why you ask me such questions?

FAITHFUL: Because I saw you forward to talk, and because I knew not that you had aught else but notion. Besides, to tell you all the truth, I have heard of you that you are a man whose religion lies in talk, and that your conversation gives this your mouth-profession the lie. They say you are a spot among Christians, and that religion fareth the worse for your ungodly conversation; that some have already stumbled at your wicked ways, and that more are in danger of being destroyed thereby: your religion, and an ale-house, and covetousness, and uncleanness, and swearing, and lying, and vain company-keeping, etc., will stand together. The proverb is true of you which is said of a harlot, to wit, "That she is a shame to all women:" so are you a shame to all professors.

TALKATIVE: Since you are so ready to take up reports, and to judge so rashly as you do, I cannot but conclude you are some peevish or melancholy man, not fit to be discoursed with; and so adieu.

Then up came Christian, and said to his brother, I told you how it would happen; your words and his lusts could not agree. He had rather leave your company than reform his life. But he is gone, as I said: let him go; the loss is no man's but his own. He has saved us the trouble of going from him; for he continuing (as I suppose he will do) as he is, would have been but a blot in our company: besides, the apostle says, "From such withdraw thyself."

FAITHFUL: But I am glad we had this little discourse with him; it may happen that he will think of it again: however, I have dealt plainly with him, and so am clear of his blood if he perisheth.

CHRISTIAN: You did well to talk so plainly to him as you did. There is but little of this faithful dealing with men now-a-days, and that makes religion to stink so in the nostrils of many as it doth; for they are these talkative fools, whose religion is only in word, and who are debauched and vain in their conversation, that (being so much admitted into the fellowship of the godly) do puzzle the world, blemish Christianity, and grieve the sincere. I wish that all men would deal with such as you have done; then should they either be made more conformable to religion, or the company of saints would be too hot for them. Then did Faithful say,

"How Talkative at first lifts up his plumes!
How bravely doth he speak! How he presumes
To drive down all before him! But so soon
As Faithful talks of heart-work, like the moon
That's past the full, into the wane he goes;
And so will all but he that heart-work know."

Thus they went on, talking of what they had seen by the way, and so made that way easy, which would otherwise no doubt have been tedious to them, for now they went through a wilderness.

# 23

# EVANGELIST REUNION

NOW WHEN they were got almost quite out of this wilderness, Faithful chanced to cast his eye back, and espied one coming after them, and he knew him. Oh! said Faithful to his brother, who comes yonder? Then Christian looked, and said, It is my good friend Evangelist. Aye, and my good friend too, said Faithful, for 'twas he that set me on the way to the gate. Now was Evangelist come up unto them, and thus saluted them.

EVANGELIST: Peace be with you, dearly beloved, and peace be to your helpers.

CHRISTIAN: Welcome, welcome, my good Evangelist: the sight of thy countenance brings to my remembrance thy ancient kindness and unwearied labors for my eternal good.

FAITHFUL: And a thousand times welcome, said good Faithful, thy company, O sweet Evangelist; how desirable is it to us poor pilgrims!

EVANGELIST: Then said Evangelist, How hath it fared with you, my friends, since the time of our last parting? What have you met with, and how have you behaved yourselves?

Then Christian and Faithful told him of all things that had happened to them in the way; and how, and with what difficulty, they had arrived to that place.

Right glad am I, said Evangelist, not that you have met with trials, but that you have been victors, and for that you have, notwithstanding many weaknesses, continued in the way to this very day.

I say, right glad am I of this thing, and that for mine own sake and yours: I have sowed, and you have reaped; and the day is coming, when "both he that soweth, and they that reap, shall rejoice together," that is, if you hold out: "for in due season ye shall reap, if ye faint not." The crown is before you, and it is an incorruptible one; "so run that ye may obtain it." Some there be that set out for this crown, and after they have gone far for it, another comes in and takes it from them: "hold fast, therefore, that you have; let no man take your crown." You are not yet out of the gunshot of the devil; "you have not resisted unto blood, striving against sin." Let the kingdom be always before you, and believe steadfastly concerning the things that are invisible. Let nothing that is on this side the other world get within you. And, above all, look well to your own hearts and to the lusts thereof; for they are "deceitful above all things, and desperately wicked." Set your faces like a flint; you have all power in heaven and earth on your side.

*John 4: 36*

*Galatians 6:9*

*1 Corinthians 9:24–27*

*Revelation 3:11*

CHRISTIAN: Then Christian thanked him for his exhortations; but told him withal, that they would have him speak farther to them for their help the rest of the way; and the rather, for that they well knew that he was a prophet, and could tell them of things that might happen unto them, and also how they might resist and overcome them. To which request Faithful also consented. So Evangelist began as followeth.

EVANGELIST: My sons, you have heard in the word of the truth of the Gospel, that you must "through many tribulations enter into the kingdom of heaven;" and again, that "in every city, bonds and afflictions abide you;" and therefore you cannot expect that you should go long on your pilgrimage without them, in some sort or other. You have found something of the truth of these testimonies upon you already, and more will immediately follow: for now, as you see, you are almost out of this wilderness, and therefore you will soon come into a town that you will by and by see before you; and in that town you will be hardly beset with enemies, who will strain hard but they will kill you; and be you sure that one or both of you must seal the testimony which you hold, with blood; but "be you faithful unto death, and the King will give you a crown of life." He that shall die there, although his death will be unnatural, and his pain, perhaps, great, he will yet have the better of his fellow; not only because he will be arrived at the Celestial City soonest, but because he will escape many miseries that the other will meet with in the rest of his journey. But when you are come to the town, and shall find fulfilled what I have here related, then remember your friend, and quit yourselves like men, and "commit the keeping of your souls to God in well doing, as unto a faithful Creator."

# 24

# Vanity Fair,
# Hubbub in the Fair,
# In the Cage

THEN I saw in my dream, that when they were got out of the wilderness, they presently saw a town before them, and the name of that town is Vanity; and at the town there is a fair kept, called Vanity Fair. It is kept all the year long. It beareth the name of Vanity Fair, because the town where it is kept is lighter than vanity, and also because all that is there sold, or that cometh thither, is vanity; as is the saying of the wise, "All that cometh is vanity."

*Psalm 62:9*

*Ecclesiastes 11:8
(see also 1:2–14;
2:11–17)*

*Isaiah 40:17*

This fair is no new-erected business but a thing of ancient standing. I will show you the original of it.

Almost five thousand years ago there were pilgrims walking to the Celestial City, as these two honest persons are: and Beelzebub, Apollyon, and Legion, with their companions, perceiving by the path that the pilgrims made, that their way to the city lay through this town of Vanity, they contrived here to set up a fair; a fair wherein should be sold all sorts of vanity, and that it should last all the year long. Therefore, at this fair are all such merchandise sold as houses, lands, trades, places, honors, preferments, titles, countries, kingdoms, lusts, pleasures; and delights of all sorts, as harlots, wives, husbands, children, masters, servants, lives, blood, bodies, souls, silver, gold, pearls, precious stones, and what not.

And moreover, at this fair there is at all times to be seen jugglings, cheats, games, plays, fools, apes, knaves, and rogues, and that of every kind.

Here are to be seen, too, and that for nothing, thefts, murders, adulteries, false-swearers, and that of a blood-red color.

And, as in other fairs of less moment, there are the several rows and streets under their proper names, where such and such wares are vended; so here, likewise, you have the proper places, rows, streets, (namely, countries and kingdoms,) where the wares of this fair are soonest to be found. Here is the Britain Row, the French Row, the Italian Row, the Spanish Row, the German Row, where several sorts of vanities are to be sold. But, as in other fairs, some one commodity is as the chief of all the fair; so the ware of Rome and her merchandise is greatly promoted in this fair; only our English nation, with some others, have taken a dislike thereat.

Now, as I said, the way to the Celestial City lies just through this town, where this lusty fair is kept; and he that will go to the city, and yet not go through this town, *1 Corinthians 4:10* "must needs go out of the world." The Prince of princes himself, when here, went through this town to his own country, and that upon a fair-day too; yea, and, as I think, it was Beelzebub, the chief lord of this fair, that invited him to buy of his vanities, yea, would have made him lord of the fair, would he but have done him reverence as he went through the town. Yea, because he was such a person of honor, Beelzebub had him from street to street, and showed him all the kingdoms of the world in a little time, that he might, if possible, allure that blessed One to cheapen and buy some of his vanities; but he had no mind to the merchandise, and therefore left the town, without laying out so much as one farthing upon these vanities. This fair, therefore, is an ancient thing, of long standing, and a very great fair.

*Matthew 4:8–9*
*Luke 4:5–7*

Now, these pilgrims, as I said, must needs go through this fair. Well, so they did; but behold, even as they entered into the fair, all the people in the fair were moved; and the town itself, as it were, in a hubbub about them, and that for several reasons: for,

First, The Pilgrims were clothed with such kind of raiment as was diverse from the raiment of any that traded in that fair. The people, therefore, of the fair made a

*1 Corinthians 4:9–10*

great gazing upon them: some said they were fools; some, they were bedlams; and some, they were outlandish men.

Secondly, And as they wondered at their apparel, so they did likewise at their speech; for few could understand what they said. They naturally spoke the language of Canaan; but they that kept the fair were the men of this world: so that from one end of the fair to the other,

*1 Corinthians 2:7–8*

they seemed barbarians each to the other.

Thirdly, But that which did not a little amuse the merchandisers was, that these pilgrims set very light by all their wares. They cared not so much as to look upon them; and if they called upon them to buy, they would put their fingers in their ears, and cry, "Turn away mine

*Psalm 119:37*

eyes from beholding vanity," and look upward, signify-

*Philippians 3:20–21*

ing that their trade and traffic was in heaven.

One chanced, mockingly, beholding the carriage of the men, to say unto them, "What will ye buy?" But they,

*Proverbs 23:23*

looking gravely upon him, said, "We buy the truth." At that there was an occasion taken to despise the men the more; some mocking, some taunting, some speaking reproachfully, and some calling upon others to smite them. At last, things came to an hubbub and great stir in the fair, insomuch that all order was confounded. Now was word presently brought to the great one of the fair, who quickly came down, and deputed some of his most trusty friends to take those men into examination about whom the fair was almost overturned. So the men were brought to examination; and they that sat upon them asked them whence they came, whither they went, and what they did there in such an unusual garb. The men told them they were pilgrims and strangers in the world, and that they were going to their own country, which was the

*Hebrews 11:13-16*

heavenly Jerusalem; and that they had given no occasion to the men of the town, nor yet to the merchandisers, thus to abuse them, and to let them in their journey, except it was for that, when one asked them what they would buy, they said they would buy the truth. But they that were appointed to examine them did not believe them to be any other than bedlams and mad, or else such as came to put all things into a confusion in the fair. Therefore they took them and beat them, and besmeared them with dirt, and then put them into the cage, that they might be made a spectacle to all the men of the fair.

There, therefore, they lay for some time, and were made the objects of any man's sport, or malice, or revenge; the great one of the fair laughing still at all that befell them. But the men being patient, and "not rendering railing for railing, but contrariwise blessing," and giving good words for bad, and kindness for injuries done, some men in the fair, that were more observing and less prejudiced than the rest, began to check and blame the baser sort for their continual abuses done by them to the men. They, therefore, in an angry manner let fly at them again, counting them as bad as the men in the cage, and telling them that they seemed confederates, and should be made partakers of their misfortunes. The others replied that, for aught they could see, the men were quiet and sober, and intended nobody any harm; and that there were many that traded in their fair that were more worthy to be put into the cage, yea, and pillory too, than were the men that they had abused. Thus, after divers words had passed on both sides, (the men behaving themselves all the while very wisely and soberly before them,) they fell to some blows among themselves, and did harm one to another. Then were these two poor men brought before their examiners again, and were charged as being guilty of the late hubbub that had been in the fair. So they beat them pitifully, and hanged irons upon them, and led them in chains up and down the fair, for an example and terror to others, lest any should speak in their behalf, or join themselves unto them. But Christian and Faithful behaved themselves yet more wisely, and received the ignominy and shame that was cast upon them with so much meekness and patience, that it won to their side (though but few in comparison of the rest) several of the men in the fair. This put the other party yet into a greater rage, insomuch that they concluded the death of these two men. Wherefore they threatened that neither cage nor irons should serve their turn, but that they should die for the abuse they had done, and for deluding the men of the fair.

Then were they remanded to the cage again, until further order should be taken with them. So they put them in, and made their feet fast in the stocks.

Here, also, they called again to mind what they had heard from their faithful friend Evangelist, and were the more confirmed in their way and sufferings by what he told them would happen to them. They also now comforted each other, that whose lot it was to suffer, even he should have the best of it: therefore each man secretly wished that he might have that preferment. But committing themselves to the all-wise disposal of Him that ruleth all things, with much content they abode in the condition in which they were, until they should be otherwise disposed of.

# 25

# TRIAL OF FAITHFUL, DEFENSE & DEATH

THEN A convenient time being appointed, they brought them forth to their trial, in order to their condemnation. When the time was come, they were brought before their enemies and arraigned. The judge's name was Lord Hate-good; their indictment was one and the same in substance, though somewhat varying in form; the contents whereof was this: "That they were enemies to, and disturbers of, the trade; that they had made commotions and divisions in the town, and had won a party to their own most dangerous opinions, in contempt of the law of their prince."

Then Faithful began to answer, that he had only set himself against that which had set itself against Him that is higher than the highest. And, said he, as for disturbance, I make none, being myself a man of peace: the parties that were won to us, were won by beholding our truth and innocence, and they are only turned from the worse to the better. And as to the king you talk of, since he is Beelzebub, the enemy of our Lord, I defy him and all his angels.

Then proclamation was made, that they that had ought to say for their lord the king against the prisoner at the bar, should forthwith appear, and give in their evidence. So there came in three witnesses, to wit, Envy, Superstition, and Pickthank. They were then asked if they knew the prisoner at the bar; and what they had to say for their lord the king against him.

Then stood forth Envy, and said to this effect: My lord, I have known this man a long time, and will attest upon my oath before this honorable bench, that he is—

JUDGE: Hold; give him his oath.

So they sware him. Then he said, My lord, this man, notwithstanding his plausible name, is one of the vilest men in our country; he neither regardeth prince nor people, law nor custom, but doeth all that he can to possess all men with certain of his disloyal notions, which he in the general calls principles of faith and holiness. And in particular, I heard him once myself affirm, that Christianity and the customs of our town of Vanity were diametrically opposite, and could not be reconciled. By which saying, my lord, he doth at once not only condemn all our laudable doings, but us in the doing of them.

Then did the judge say to him, Hast thou any more to say?

ENVY: My lord, I could say much more, only I would not be tedious to the court. Yet if need be, when the other gentlemen have given in their evidence, rather than any thing shall be wanting that will dispatch him, I will enlarge my testimony against him. So he was bid to stand by.

Then they called Superstition, and bid him look upon the prisoner. They also asked, what he could say for their lord the king against him. Then they sware him; so he began.

SUPERSTITION: My lord, I have no great acquaintance with this man, nor do I desire to have further knowledge of him. However, this

I know, that he is a very pestilent fellow, from some discourse that I had with him the other day, in this town; for then, talking with him, I heard him say, that our religion was naught, and such by which a man could by no means please God. Which saying of his, my lord, your lordship very well knows what necessarily thence will follow, to wit, that we still do worship in vain, are yet in our sins, and finally shall be damned: and this is that which I have to say.

Then was Pickthank sworn, and bid say what he knew in the behalf of their lord the king against the prisoner at the bar.

PICKTHANK: My lord, and you gentlemen all, this fellow I have known of a long time, and have heard him speak things that ought not to be spoken; for he hath railed on our noble prince Beelzebub, and hath spoken contemptibly of his honorable friends, whose names are, the Lord Old Man, the Lord Carnal Delight, the Lord Luxurious, the Lord Desire of Vain Glory, my old Lord Lechery, Sir Having Greedy, with all the rest of our nobility: and he hath said, moreover, that if all men were of his mind, if possible, there is not one of these noblemen should have any longer a being in this town. Besides, he hath not been afraid to rail on you, my lord, who are now appointed to be his judge, calling you an ungodly villain, with many other such like vilifying terms, with which he hath bespattered most of the gentry of our town.

When this Pickthank had told his tale, the judge directed his speech to the prisoner at the bar, saying, Thou runagate, heretic, and traitor, hast thou heard what these honest gentlemen have witnessed against thee?

FAITHFUL: May I speak a few words in my own defence?

JUDGE: Sirrah, sirrah, thou deservest to live no longer, but to be slain immediately upon the place; yet, that all men may see our gentleness towards thee, let us hear what thou, vile runagate, hast to say.

FAITHFUL: 1. I say, then, in answer to what Mr. Envy hath spoken, I never said aught but this, that what rule, or laws, or custom, or people, were flat against the word of God, are diametrically opposite to Christianity. If I have said amiss in this, convince me of my error, and I am ready here before you to make my recantation.

2. As to the second, to wit, Mr. Superstition, and his charge against me, I said only this, that in the worship of God there is required a divine faith; but there can be no divine faith without a divine revelation of the will of God. Therefore, whatever is thrust into the worship of God that is not agreeable to divine revelation, cannot be done but by a human faith; which faith will not be profitable to eternal life.

3. As to what Mr. Pickthank hath said, I say, (avoiding terms, as that I am said to rail, and the like,) that the prince of this town, with all the rabblement, his attendants, by this gentleman named, are more fit for a being in hell than in this town and country. And so the Lord have mercy upon me.

Then the judge called to the jury, (who all this while stood by to hear and observe,) Gentlemen of the jury, you see this man about whom so great an uproar hath been made in this town; you have also heard what these worthy gentlemen have witnessed against him; also, you have heard his reply and confession: it lieth now in your breasts to hang him, or save his life; but yet I think meet to instruct you in our law.

There was an act made in the days of Pharaoh the

Great, servant to our prince, that, lest those of a contrary religion should multiply and grow too strong for him, their males should be thrown into the river. There was also an act made in the days of Nebuchadnezzar the Great, another of his servants, that whoever would not fall down and worship his golden image, should be thrown into a fiery furnace. There was also an act made in the days of Darius, that whoso for some time called upon any god but him, should be cast into the lion's den. Now, the substance of these laws this rebel has broken, not only in thought, (which is not to be borne,) but also in word and deed; which must, therefore, needs be intolerable.

*Exodus 1:22*

*Daniel 3:6*

*Daniel 6:7*

For that of Pharaoh, his law was made upon a supposition to prevent mischief, no crime being yet apparent; but here is a crime apparent. For the second and third, you see he disputeth against our religion; and for the treason that he hath already confessed, he deserveth to die the death.

Then went the jury out, whose names were Mr. Blindman, Mr. No-good, Mr. Malice, Mr. Love-lust, Mr. Live-loose, Mr. Heady, Mr. High-mind, Mr. Enmity, Mr. Liar, Mr. Cruelty, Mr. Hate-light, and Mr. Implacable; who every one gave in his private verdict against him among themselves, and afterwards unanimously concluded to bring him in guilty before the judge. And first among themselves, Mr. Blindman, the foreman, said, I see clearly that this man is a heretic. Then said Mr. No-good, Away with such a fellow from the earth. Aye, said Mr. Malice, for I hate the very looks of him. Then said Mr. Love-lust, I could never endure him. Nor I, said Mr. Live-loose, for he would always be condemning my way. Hang him, hang him, said Mr. Heady. A sorry scrub, said Mr. High-mind. My heart riseth against him, said Mr. Enmity. He is a rogue, said Mr. Liar. Hanging is too good for him, said Mr. Cruelty. Let us dispatch him out of the way, said Mr. Hate-light. Then said Mr. Implacable, Might I have all the world given me, I could not be reconciled to him; therefore let us forthwith bring him in guilty of death.

And so they did; therefore he was presently condemned to be had from the place where he was, to the place from whence he came, and there to be put to the most cruel death that could be invented.

They therefore brought him out, to do with him according to their law; and first they scourged him, then they buffeted him, then they lanced his flesh with knives; after that, they stoned him with stones, then pricked him with their swords; and last of all, they burned him to ashes at the stake. Thus came Faithful to his end.

Now I saw, that there stood behind the multitude a chariot and a couple of horses waiting for Faithful, who (so soon as his adversaries had dispatched him) was taken up into it, and straightway was carried up through the clouds with sound of trumpet, the nearest way to the celestial gate.

> Brave Faithful, bravely done in word and deed
> Judge, witnesses and jury have instead of overcoming thee
> But shown their rage and they are dead
> Thou wilt live from age to age.

# 26

# HOPEFUL & BY-ENDS,
# BY-ENDS' FRIENDS

B UT AS for Christian, he had some respite, and was
remanded back to prison: so he there remained for a
space. But he who overrules all things, having the power
of their rage in his own hand, so wrought it about, that
Christian for that time escaped them, and went his way.

And as he went, he sang, saying,

"Well, Faithful, thou hast faithfully profest
Unto thy Lord, with whom thou shalt be blest,
When faithless ones, with all their vain delights,
Are crying out under their hellish plights:
Sing, Faithful, sing, and let thy name survive;
For though they killed thee, thou art yet alive."

Now I saw in my dream, that Christian went not
forth alone; for there was one whose name was Hopeful,
(being so made by the beholding of Christian and
Faithful in their words and behavior, in their sufferings
at the fair,) who joined himself unto him, and entering
into a brotherly covenant, told him that he would be
his companion. Thus one died to bear testimony to the
truth, and another rises out of his ashes to be a companion with Christian in his pilgrimage. This Hopeful also
told Christian, that there were many more of the men in
the fair that would take their time, and follow after.

So I saw, that quickly after they were got out of the

fair, they overtook one that was going before them, whose name was By-ends; so they said to him, What country-man, sir? and how far go you this way? He told them, that he came from the town of Fair-speech, and he was going to the Celestial City; but told them not his name.

From Fair-speech? said Christian; is there any good that lives there?

*Proverbs 26:25*

BY-ENDS: Yes, said By-ends, I hope so.

CHRISTIAN: Pray, sir, what may I call you? said Christian.

BY-ENDS: I am a stranger to you, and you to me: if you be going this way, I shall be glad of your company; if not, I must be content.

CHRISTIAN: This town of Fair-speech, said Christian, I have heard of; and, as I remember, they say it's a wealthy place.

BY-ENDS: Yes, I will assure you that it is; and I have very many rich kindred there.

CHRISTIAN: Pray, who are your kindred there, if a man may be so bold?

BY-ENDS: Almost the whole town; and in particular my Lord Turn-about, my Lord Time-server, my Lord Fair-speech, from whose ancestors that town first took its name; also, Mr. Smooth-man, Mr. Facing-both-ways, Mr. Any-thing; and the parson of our parish, Mr. Two-tongues, was my mother's own brother, by father's side; and, to tell you the truth, I am become a gentle-man of good quality; yet my great-grandfather was but a waterman, looking one way and rowing another, and I got most of my estate by the same occupation.

CHRISTIAN: Are you a married man.

BY-ENDS: Yes, and my wife is a very virtuous woman, the daughter of a virtuous woman; she was my Lady Feigning's daughter; therefore she came of a very honorable family, and is arrived to such a pitch of breeding, that she knows how to carry it to all, even to prince and peasant. 'Tis true, we somewhat differ in religion from those of the stricter sort, yet but in two small points: First, we never strive against wind and tide. Secondly, we are always most zealous when religion goes in his silver slippers; we love much to walk with him in the street, if the sun shines and the people applaud him.

Then Christian stepped a little aside to his fellow Hopeful, saying, it runs in my mind that this is one By-ends, of Fair-speech; and if it be he, we have as very a knave in our company as dwelleth in all these parts. Then said Hopeful, Ask him; methinks he should not be ashamed of his name. So Christian came up with him again, and said, Sir, you talk as if you knew something more than all the world doth; and, if I take not my mark amiss, I deem I have half a guess of you. Is not your name Mr. By-ends of Fair-speech?

BY-ENDS: This is not my name, but indeed it is a nickname that is given me by some that cannot abide me, and I must be content to bear it as a reproach, as other good men have borne theirs before me.

CHRISTIAN: But did you never give an occasion to men to call you by this name?

BY-ENDS: Never, never! The worst that ever I did to give them an occasion to give me this name was, that I had always the luck to jump in my judgment with the present way of the times, whatever it was, and my chance was to get thereby: but if things are thus cast upon me, let me count them a blessing; but let not the malicious load me therefore with reproach.

CHRISTIAN: I thought, indeed, that you were the man that I heard of; and to tell you what I think, I fear this name belongs to you more properly than you are willing we should think it doth.

BY-ENDS: Well if you will thus imagine, I cannot help it; you shall find me a fair company-keeper, if you will still admit me your associate.

CHRISTIAN: If you will go with us, you must go against wind and tide; the which, I perceive, is against your opinion: you must also own Religion in his rags, as well as when in his silver slippers; and stand by him, too, when bound in irons, as well as when he walketh the streets with applause.

BY-ENDS: You must not impose, nor lord it over my faith; leave me to my liberty, and let me go with you.

CHRISTIAN: Not a step farther, unless you will do, in what I propound, as we.

Then said By-ends, I shall never desert my old principles, since they are harmless and profitable. If I may not go with you, I must do as I did before you overtook me, even go by myself, until some overtake me that will be glad of my company.

Now I saw in my dream, that Christian and Hopeful forsook him, and kept their distance before him; but one of them, looking back, saw three men following Mr. By-ends; and, behold, as they came up with him, he made them a very low congee; and they also gave him a compliment. The men's names were, Mr. Hold-the-world, Mr. Money-love, and Mr. Save-all, men that Mr. By-ends had formerly been acquainted with; for in their minority they were schoolfellows, and taught by one Mr. Gripeman, a schoolmaster in Lovegain, which is a market-town in the county of Coveting, in the North. This Schoolmaster taught them the art of getting, either by violence, cozenage, flattering, lying, or by putting on a guise of religion; and these four gentlemen had attained much of the art of their master, so that they could each of them have kept such a school themselves.

Well, when they had, as I said, thus saluted each other, Mr. Money-love said to Mr. By-ends, Who are they upon the road before us? For Christian and Hopeful were yet within view.

BY-ENDS: They are a couple of far country-men, that, after their mode, are going on pilgrimage.

MR. MONEY-LOVE: Alas! why did they not stay, that we might have had their good company? for they, and we, and you, sir, I hope, are all going on pilgrimage.

BY-ENDS: We are so, indeed; but the men before us are so rigid, and love so much their own notions, and do also so lightly esteem the opinions of others, that let a man be ever so godly, yet if he jumps not with them in all things, they thrust him quite out of their company.

MR. SAVE-ALL: That is bad; but we read of some that are righteous overmuch, and such men's rigidness prevails with them to judge and condemn all but themselves. But I pray, what, and how many, were the things wherein you differed?

BY-ENDS: Why, they, after their headstrong manner, conclude that it is their duty to rush on their journey all weathers, and I am for waiting for wind and tide. They are for hazarding all for God at a clap; and I am for taking all advantages to secure my life and estate. They are for holding their notions, though all other men be against them; but I am for religion in what, and so far as the times and my safety will bear it. They are for religion when in rags and contempt; but I am for him when he walks in his silver slippers, in the sunshine, and with applause.

MR. HOLD-THE-WORLD: Aye, and hold you there still, good Mr. By-ends; for, for my part, I can count him but a fool, that having the liberty to keep what he has, shall be so unwise as to lose it. Let us be wise as serpents. It is best to make hay while the sun shines. You see how the bee lieth still in winter, and bestirs her only when she can have profit with pleasure. God sends sometimes rain, and sometimes sunshine: if they be such fools to go through the first, yet let us be content to take fair weather along with us. For my part, I like that religion best that will stand with the security of God's good blessings unto us; for who can imagine, that is ruled by his reason, since God has bestowed upon us the good things of this life, but that he would have us keep them for his sake? Abraham and Solomon grew rich in religion; and Job says, that a good man shall lay up gold as dust; but he must not be such as the men before us, if they be as you have described them.

MR. SAVE-ALL: I think that we are all agreed in this matter; and therefore there needs no more words about it.

MR. MONEY-LOVE: No, there needs no more words about this matter, indeed; for he that believes neither Scripture nor reason, (and you see we have both on our side,) neither knows his own liberty nor seeks his own safety.

BY-ENDS: My brethren, we are, as you see, going all on pilgrimage; and for our better diversion from things that are bad, give me leave to propound unto you this question.

Suppose a man, a minister, or a tradesman, etc., should have an advantage lie before him to get the good blessings of this life, yet so as that he can by no means come by them, except, in appearance at least, he becomes extraordinary zealous in some points of religion that he meddled not with before; may he not use this means to attain his end, and yet be a right honest man?

# 27

# MONEY-LOVE VS.

# CHRISTIAN

MR. MONEY-LOVE: I see the bottom of your question; and with these gentlemen's good leave, I will endeavor to shape you an answer. And first, to speak to your question as it concerneth a minister himself: suppose a minister, a worthy man, possessed but of a very small benefice, and has in his eye a greater, more fat and plump by far; he has also now an opportunity of getting it, yet so as by being more studious, by preaching more frequently and zealously, and, because the temper of the people requires it, by altering of some of his principles; for my part, I see no reason why a man may not do this, provided he has a call, aye, and more a great deal besides, and yet be an honest man. For why?

His desire of a greater benefice is lawful, (this cannot be contradicted,) since it is set before him by Providence; so then he may get it if he can, making no question for conscience' sake.

Besides, his desire after that benefice makes him more studious, a more zealous preacher, etc., and so makes him a better man, yea, makes him better improve his parts, which is according to the mind of God.

Now, as for his complying with the temper of his people, by desenting, to serve them, some of his principles, this argueth,

1. That he is of a self-denying temper.

2. Of a sweet and winning deportment. And,

3. So more fit for the ministerial function.

I conclude, then, that a minister that changes a small for a great, should not, for so doing, be judged as covetous; but rather, since he is improved in his parts and industry thereby, be counted as one that pursues his call, and the opportunity put into his hand to do good.

And now to the second part of the question, which concerns the tradesman you mentioned. Suppose such an one to have but a poor employ in the world, but by becoming religious he may mend his market, perhaps get a rich wife, or more and far better customers to his shop; for my part, I see no reason but this may be lawfully done. For why?

To become religious is a virtue, by what means soever a man becomes so.

Nor is it unlawful to get a rich wife, or more custom to my shop.

Besides, the man that gets these by becoming religious, gets that which is good of them that are good, by becoming good himself; so then here is a good wife, and good customers, and good gain, and all these by becoming religious, which is good: therefore, to become religious to get all these is a good and profitable design.

This answer, thus made by Mr. Money-love to Mr. By-ends' question, was highly applauded by them all; wherefore they concluded, upon the whole, that it was most wholesome and advantageous. And because, as they thought, no man was able to contradict it; and because Christian and Hopeful were yet within call, they jointly agreed to assault them with the question as soon as they overtook them; and the rather, because they had opposed Mr. By-ends before. So they called after them, and they stopped and stood still till they came up to them; but they concluded, as they went, that not Mr. By-ends, but old Mr. Hold-the-world should propound the question to them, because, as they supposed, their answer to him would be without the remainder of that heat that was kindled betwixt Mr. By-ends and them at their parting a little before.

So they came up to each other, and after a short salutation, Mr. Hold-the-world propounded the question to Christian and his fellow, and then bid them to answer if they could.

Then said Christian, Even a babe in religion may answer ten thousand such questions. For if it be unlawful to follow Christ for loaves, as it is; how much more *John 6:26* abominable is it to make of him and religion a stalking-horse to get and enjoy the world! Nor do we find any other than heathens, hypocrites, devils, and wizards, that are of this opinion.

Heathens: for when Hamor and Shechem had a mind to the daughter and cattle of Jacob, and saw that there was no way for them to come at them but by being circumcised, they said to their companions, If every male of us be circumcised, as they are circumcised, shall not their cattle, and their substance, and every beast of theirs be ours? Their daughters and their cattle were that which they sought to obtain, and their religion the stalking-horse they made use of to come at them. *Genesis 34:20–24*

The hypocritical Pharisees were also of this religion: long prayers were their pretence, but to get widows' houses was their intent; and greater damnation was from God their judgment.

Luke 20:46–47

Judas the devil was also of this religion: he was religious for the bag, that he might be possessed of what was put therein; but he was lost, cast away, and the very son of perdition.

Simon the wizard was of this religion too; for he would have had the Holy Ghost, that he might have got money therewith: and his sentence from Peter's mouth was according.

Acts 8:19–22

Neither will it go out of my mind, but that that man who takes up religion for the world, will throw away religion for the world; for so surely as Judas resigned the world in becoming religious, so surely did he also sell religion and his Master for the same. To answer the question, therefore, affirmatively, as I perceive you have done, and to accept of, as authentic, such answer, is heathenish, hypocritical, and devilish; and your reward will be according to your works.

Then they stood staring one upon another, but had not wherewith to answer Christian. Hopeful also approved of the soundness of Christian's answer; so there was a great silence among them. Mr. By-ends and his company also staggered and kept behind, that Christian and Hopeful might outgo them. Then said Christian to his fellow, If these men cannot stand before the sentence of men, what will they do with the sentence of God? And if they are mute when dealt with by vessels of clay, what will they do when they shall be rebuked by the flames of a devouring fire?

# 28

# HILL LUCRE & DEMAS

THEN CHRISTIAN and Hopeful outwent them again, and went till they came at a delicate plain, called Ease, where they went with much content; but that plain was but narrow, so they were quickly got over it. Now at the farther side of that plain was a little hill, called Lucre, and in that hill a silver-mine, which some of them that had formerly gone that way, because of the rarity of it, had turned aside to see; but going too near the brim of the pit, the ground, being deceitful under them, broke, and they were slain: some also had been maimed there, and could not, to their dying day, be their own men again.

Then I saw in my dream, that a little off the road, over against the silver-mine, stood Demas (gentleman-like) to call passengers to come and see; who said to Christian and his fellow, Ho! turn aside hither, and I will show you a thing.

CHRISTIAN: What thing so deserving as to turn us out of the way to see it?

DEMAS: Here is a silver-mine, and some digging in it for treasure; if you will come, with a little pains you may richly provide for yourselves.

HOPEFUL: Then said Hopeful, let us go see.

CHRISTIAN: Not I, said Christian: I have heard of this place before now, and how many there have been slain; and besides, that treasure is a snare to those that seek it, for it hindereth them in their pilgrimage.

Then Christian called to Demas, saying, Is not the place dangerous? Hath it not hindered many in their pilgrimage?

*Hosea 9:6*

DEMAS: Not very dangerous, except to those that are careless; but withal he blushed as he spake.

CHRISTIAN: Then said Christian to Hopeful, Let us not stir a step, but still keep on our way.

HOPEFUL: I will warrant you, when By-ends comes up, if he hath the same invitation as we, he will turn in thither to see.

CHRISTIAN: No doubt thereof, for his principles lead him that way, and a hundred to one but he dies there.

DEMAS: Then Demas called again, saying, But will you not come over and see?

CHRISTIAN: Then Christian roundly answered, saying, Demas, thou art an enemy to the right ways of the Lord of this way, and hast been already condemned for thine own turning aside, by one of his Majesty's judges ; and why seekest thou to bring us into the like condemnation? Besides, if we at all turn aside, our Lord the King will certainly hear thereof, and will there put us to shame, where we would stand with boldness before him.

*2 Timothy 4:10*

Demas cried again, that he also was one of their fraternity; and that if they would tarry a little, he also himself would walk with them.

CHRISTIAN: Then said Christian, What is thy name? Is it not the same by which I have called thee?

DEMAS: Yes, my name is Demas; I am the son of Abraham.

CHRISTIAN: I know you; Gehazi was your great-grandfather, and Judas your father, and you have trod in their steps; it is but a devilish prank that thou usest: thy father was hanged for a traitor, and thou deservest no better reward. Assure thyself, that when we come to the King, we will tell him of this thy behavior. Thus they went their way.

*2 Kings 5:20–27*
*Matthew 26:14–15;*
*27:3–5*

By this time By-ends and his companions were come again within sight, and they at the first beck went over to Demas. Now, whether they fell into the pit by looking over the brink thereof, or whether they went down to dig, or whether they were smothered in the bottom by the damps that commonly arise, of these things I am not certain; but this I observed, that they were never seen again in the way. Then sang Christian,

"By-ends and silver Demas both agree;
One calls, the other runs, that he may be
A sharer in his lucre: so these two
Take up in this world, and no farther go."

Now I saw that, just on the other side of this plain, the pilgrims came to a place where stood an old monument, hard by the highway-side, at the sight of which they were both concerned, because of the strangeness of the form thereof; for it seemed to them as if it had been a woman transformed into the shape of a pillar. Here, therefore, they stood looking and looking upon it, but could not for a time tell what they should make thereof. At last Hopeful espied, written above upon the head thereof, a writing in an unusual hand; but he being no scholar, called to Christian (for he was learned) to see if he could pick out the meaning: so he came, and after a little laying of letters together, he found the same to be this, "Remember Lot's wife." So he read it to his fellow; after which they both concluded that that was the pillar of salt into which Lot's wife was turned, for her looking back with a covetous heart when she was going from Sodom for safety. Which sudden and amazing sight gave them occasion for this discourse.

*Genesis 19:26*

CHRISTIAN: Ah, my brother, this is a seasonable sight: it came opportunely to us after the invitation which Demas gave us to come over to view the hill Lucre; and had we gone over, as he desired us, and as thou wast inclined to do, my brother, we had, for aught I know, been made, like this woman, a spectacle for those that shall come after to behold.

HOPEFUL: I am sorry that I was so foolish, and am made to wonder that I am not now as Lot's wife; for wherein was the difference betwixt her sin and mine? She only looked back, and I had a desire to go see. Let grace be adored; and let me be ashamed that ever such a thing should be in mine heart.

CHRISTIAN: Let us take notice of what we see here, for our help from time to come. This woman escaped one judgment, for she fell not by the destruction of Sodom; yet she was destroyed by another, as we see: she is turned into a pillar of salt.

HOPEFUL: True, and she may be to us both caution and example; caution, that we should shun her sin; or a sign of what judgment will overtake such as shall not be prevented by this

caution: so Korah, Dathan, and Abiram, with the two hundred and fifty men that perished in their sin, did also become a sign or example to others to beware. But above all, I muse at one thing, to wit, how Demas and his fellows can stand so confidently yonder to look for that treasure, which this woman but for looking behind her after, (for we read not that she stepped one foot out of the way,) was turned into a pillar of

*Numbers 16:31–32; 26:9–10*

197

salt; especially since the judgment which overtook her did make her an example within sight of where they are; for they cannot choose but see her, did they but lift up their eyes.

CHRISTIAN: It is a thing to be wondered at, and it argueth that their hearts are grown desperate in the case; and I cannot tell who to compare them to so fitly, as to them that pick pockets in the presence of the judge, or that will cut purses under the gallows. It is said of the men of Sodom, that they were "sinners exceedingly," because they were sinners "before the Lord," that is, in his eyesight, and notwithstanding the kindnesses that he had shown them; for the land of Sodom was now like the garden of Eden as *Genesis 13:10–13* heretofore. This, therefore, provoked him the more to jealousy, and made their plague as hot as the fire of the Lord out of heaven could make it. And it is most rationally to be concluded, that such, even such as these are, that shall sin in the sight, yea, and that too in despite of such examples that are set continually before them, to caution them to the contrary, must be partakers of severest judgments.

HOPEFUL: Doubtless thou hast said the truth; but what a mercy is it, that neither thou, but especially I, am not made myself this example! This ministereth occasion to us to thank God, to fear before him, and always to remember Lot's wife.

*Psalm 65:9*
*Revelation 22:1*
*Ezekiel 47:1–9*

I saw then that they went on their way to a pleasant river, which David the king called "the river of God;" but John, "the river of the water of life." Now their way lay just upon the bank of this river: here, therefore, Christian and his companion walked with great delight;

they drank also of the water of the river, which was pleasant and enlivening to their weary spirits. Besides, on the banks of this river, on either side, were green trees with all manner of fruit; and the leaves they ate to prevent surfeits, and other diseases that are incident to those that heat their blood by travel. On either side of the river was also a meadow, curiously beautified with lilies; and it was green all the year long. In this meadow they lay down and slept, for here they might lie down safely. When they awoke they gathered again of the fruit of the trees, and drank again of the water of the river, and then lay down again to sleep. Thus they did several days and nights. Then they sang;

*Psalm 23:2*
*Isaiah 14:30*

> "Behold ye, how these Crystal Streams do glide,
> To comfort pilgrims by the highway-side.
> The meadows green, besides their fragrant smell,
> Yield dainties for them; And he that can tell
> What pleasant fruit, yea, leaves these trees do yield,
> Will soon sell all, that he may buy this field."

So when they were disposed to go on, (for they were not as yet at their journey's end,) they ate, and drank, and departed.

# 29

# By-Path Meadow,
# Giant Despair,
# Doubting Castle

NOW I beheld in my dream, that they had not jour-neyed far, but the river and the way for a time part-ed, at which they were not a little sorry; yet they durst not go out of the way. Now the way from the river was rough, and their feet tender by reason of their travels; so the souls of the pilgrims were much discouraged because of the way. Wherefore, still as they went on, they wished for a better way. Now, a little before them, there was on the left hand of the road a meadow, and a stile to go over into it, and that meadow is called By-path meadow. Then said Christian to his fellow, If this meadow lieth along by our wayside, let's go over into it. Then he went to the stile to see, and behold a path lay along by the way on the other side of the fence. It is according to my wish, said Christian; here is the easiest going; come, good Hopeful, and let us go over.

*Numbers 21:4*

HOPEFUL: But how if this path should lead us out of the way?

CHRISTIAN: That is not likely, said the other. Look, doth it not go along by the wayside?

So Hopeful, being persuaded by his fellow, went after him over the stile. When they were gone over, and were got into the path, they found it very easy for their feet; and withal, they, looking before them, espied a man walking as they did, and his name was Vain-Confidence: so they called after him, and asked him whither that way led. He said, To the Celestial Gate. Look, said Christian, did not I tell you so? by this you may see we are right. So they followed, and he went before them. But behold the night came on, and it grew very dark; so that they that went behind lost the sight of him that went before.

He therefore that went before, (Vain-Confidence by name,) not seeing the way before him, fell into a deep pit, which was on purpose there made, by the prince of those grounds, to catch vain-glorious fools withal, and *Isaiah 9:16* was dashed in pieces with his fall.

Now, Christian and his fellow heard him fall. So they called to know the matter, but there was none to answer, only they heard a groaning. Then said Hopeful, Where are we now? Then was his fellow silent, as mistrusting that he had led him out of the way; and now it began to rain, and thunder, and lighten in a most dreadful manner, and the water rose amain.

Then Hopeful groaned in himself, saying, Oh that I had kept on my way!

CHRISTIAN: Who could have thought that this path should have led us out of the way?

HOPEFUL: I was afraid on't at the very first, and therefore gave you that gentle caution. I would have spoke plainer, but that you are older than I.

CHRISTIAN: Good brother, be not offended; I am sorry I have brought thee out of the way, and that I have put thee into such imminent danger. Pray, my brother, forgive me; I did not do it of an evil intent.

HOPEFUL: Be comforted, my brother, for I forgive thee; and believe, too, that this shall be for our good.

CHRISTIAN: I am glad I have with me a merciful brother: but we must not stand here; let us try to go back again.

HOPEFUL: But, good brother, let me go before.

CHRISTIAN: No, if you please, let me go first, that if there be any danger, I may be first therein, because by my means we are both gone out of the way.

HOPEFUL: No, said Hopeful, you shall not go first, for your mind being troubled may lead you out of the way again. Then for their encouragement they heard the voice of one saying, "Let thine heart be toward the highway, even the way that thou wentest: turn again." But by this time the waters were greatly risen, by reason of which the way of going back was very dangerous. (Then I thought that it is easier going out of the way when we are in, than going in when we are out.) Yet they adventured to go back; but it was so dark, and the flood was so high, that in their going back they had like to have been drowned nine or ten times.

*Jeremiah 31:21*

Neither could they, with all the skill they had, get again to the stile that night. Wherefore at last, lighting under a little shelter, they sat down there till the day brake; but being weary, they fell asleep.

Now there was, not far from the place where they lay, a castle, called Doubting Castle, the owner whereof

was Giant Despair, and it was in his grounds they now were sleeping: wherefore he, getting up in the morning early, and walking up and down in his fields, caught Christian and Hopeful asleep in his grounds. Then with a grim and surly voice, he bid them awake, and asked them whence they were, and what they did in his grounds. They told him they were pilgrims, and that they had lost their way. Then said the giant, You have this night trespassed on me by trampling in and lying on my grounds, and therefore you must go along with me. So they were forced to go, because he was stronger than they. They also had but little to say, for they knew themselves in a fault. The giant, therefore, drove them before him, and put them into his castle, into a very dark dungeon, nasty and stinking to the spirits of these two men. Here, then, they lay from Wednesday morning till Saturday night, without one bit of bread, or drop of drink, or light, or any to ask how they did; they were, therefore, here in evil case, and were far from friends and acquaintance. Now in this place Christian had double sorrow, because it was through his unadvised counsel that they were brought into this distress.

*Psalm 88:18*

Now Giant Despair had a wife, and her name was Diffidence: so when he was gone to bed he told his wife what he had done, to wit, that he had taken a couple of prisoners, and cast them into his dungeon for trespassing on his grounds. Then he asked her also what he had best do further to them. So she asked him what they were, whence they came, and whither they were bound, and he told her. Then she counseled him, that when he arose in the morning he should beat them without mercy. So when he arose, he getteth him a grievous crab-tree cudgel, and goes down into the dungeon to them, and there first falls to rating of them as if they were dogs, although they gave him never a word of distaste. Then he falls upon them, and beats them fearfully, in such sort that they were not able to help themselves, or to turn them upon the floor. This done, he withdraws and leaves them there to condole their misery, and to mourn under their distress: so all that day they spent the time in nothing but sighs and bitter lamentations.

The next night, she, talking with her husband further about them, and understanding that they were yet alive, did advise him to counsel them to make away with themselves. So when morning was come, he goes to them in a surly manner, as before, and perceiving them to be very sore with the stripes that he had given them the day before, he told them, that since they were never like to come out of that place, their only way would be forthwith to make an end of themselves, either with knife, halter, or poison; for why, said he, should you choose to live, seeing it is attended with so much bitterness? But they desired him to let them go. With that he looked ugly upon them, and rushing to them, had doubtless made an end of them himself, but that he fell into one of his fits, (for he sometimes in sunshiny weather fell into fits,) and lost for a time the use of his hands; wherefore he withdrew, and left them as before to consider what to do. Then did the prisoners consult between themselves whether it was best to take his counsel or no; and thus they began to discourse:

CHRISTIAN: Brother, said Christian, what shall we do? The life that we now live is miserable. For my part, I know not whether it is best to live thus, or to die out of hand. My soul chooseth strangling rather than life, and the grave is more easy for me than this dungeon. Shall we be ruled by the giant?

*Job 7:15*

HOPEFUL: Indeed our present condition is dreadful, and death would be far more welcome to me than thus for ever to abide; but yet, let us consider, the Lord of the country to which we are going hath said, "Thou shalt do no murder," no, not to another man's person; much more, then, are we forbidden to take his counsel to kill ourselves. Besides, he that kills another, can but commit murder upon his body; but for one to kill himself, is to kill body and soul at once. And moreover, my brother, thou talkest of ease in the grave; but hast thou forgotten the hell whither for certain the murderers go? for "no murderer hath eternal life," etc. And let us consider again, that all the law is not in the hand of Giant Despair: others, so far as I can understand, have been taken by him as well as we, and yet have escaped out of his hands. Who knows but that God, who made the world, may cause that Giant Despair may die; or that, at some time or other, he may forget to lock us in; or that he may, in a short time, have another of his fits before us, and may lose the use of his limbs? And if ever that should come to pass again, for my part, I am resolved to pluck up the heart of a man, and to try my utmost to get from under his hand. I was a fool that I did not try to do it before. But, however, my brother, let us be patient, and endure a while: the time may come that may give us a happy release; but let us not be our own murderers. With these words Hopeful at present did moderate the mind of his brother; so they continued together in the dark that day, in their sad and doleful condition.

# 30

# CASTLE-YARD BONES, ESCAPE FROM CASTLE

WELL, TOWARDS evening the giant goes down into the dungeon again, to see if his prisoners had taken his counsel. But when he came there he found them alive; and truly, alive was all; for now, what for want of bread and water, and by reason of the wounds they received when he beat them, they could do little but breathe. But I say, he found them alive; at which he fell into a grievous rage, and told them, that seeing they had disobeyed his counsel, it should be worse with them than if they had never been born.

At this they trembled greatly, and I think that Christian fell into a swoon; but coming a little to himself again, they renewed their discourse about the giant's counsel, and whether yet they had best take it or no. Now Christian again seemed for doing it; but Hopeful made his second reply as followeth:

HOPEFUL: My brother, said he, rememberest thou not how valiant thou hast been heretofore? Apollyon could not crush thee, nor could all that thou didst hear, or see, or feel, in the Valley of the Shadow of Death. What hardship, terror, and amazement hast thou already gone through; and art thou now nothing but fears! Thou seest that I am in the dungeon with thee, a far weaker man by nature than thou art. Also this giant hath wounded me as well as thee, and hath also cut off the bread and water from my mouth, and with thee I mourn without the light. But let us exercise a little more patience. Remember how thou playedst the man at Vanity Fair, and wast neither afraid of the chain nor cage, nor yet of bloody death: wherefore let us (at least to avoid the shame that it becomes not a Christian to be found in) bear up with patience as well as we can.

Now night being come again, and the giant and his wife being in bed, she asked him concerning the prisoners, and if they had taken his counsel: to which he replied, They are sturdy rogues; they choose rather to bear all hardships than to make away with themselves. Then said she, Take them into the castle-yard to-morrow, and show them the bones and skulls of those that thou hast already dispatched, and make them believe, ere a week comes to an end, thou wilt tear them in pieces, as thou hast done their fellows before them.

So when the morning was come, the giant goes to them again, and takes them into the castle-yard, and shows them as his wife had bidden him. These, said he, were pilgrims, as you are, once, and they trespassed on my grounds, as you have done; and when I thought fit I tore them in pieces; and so within ten days I will do you: get you down to your den again. And with that he beat them all the way thither. They lay, therefore, all day on Saturday in a lamentable case, as before. Now, when night was come, and when Mrs. Diffidence and her husband the giant was got to bed, they began to renew their discourse of their prisoners; and withal, the old giant wondered that he could neither by his blows nor counsel bring them to an end. And with that his wife replied, I fear, said she, that they live in hopes that some will come to relieve them; or that they have pick-

locks about them, by the means of which they hope to escape. And sayest thou so, my dear? said the giant; I will therefore search them in the morning.

Well, on Saturday, about midnight they began to pray, and continued in prayer till almost break of day.

Now, a little before it was day, good Christian, as one half amazed, brake out into this passionate speech: What a fool, quoth he, am I, thus to lie in a stinking dungeon, when I may as well walk at liberty! I have a key in my bosom, called Promise, that will, I am persuaded, open any lock in Doubting Castle.

Then said Hopeful, That is good news; good brother, pluck it out of thy bosom, and try.

Then Christian pulled it out of his bosom, and began to try at the dungeon-door, whose bolt, as he turned the key, gave back, and the door flew open with ease, and Christian and Hopeful both came out. Then he went to the outward door that leads into the castle-yard, and with his key opened that door also. After he went to the iron gate, for that must be opened too; but that lock went desperately hard, yet the key did open it. They then thrust open the gate to make their escape with speed; but that gate, as it opened, made such a creaking, that it waked Giant Despair, who hastily rising to pursue his prisoners, felt his limbs to fail, for his fits took him again, so that he could by no means go after them. Then they went on, and came to the King's highway, and so were safe, because they were out of his jurisdiction.

Now, when they were gone over the stile, they began to contrive with themselves what they should do at that stile, to prevent those that shall come after from falling into the hands of Giant Despair. So they consented to erect there a pillar, and to engrave upon the side thereof this sentence: "Over this stile is the way to Doubting Castle, which is kept by Giant Despair, who despiseth the King of the Celestial country, and seeks to destroy his holy pilgrims." Many, therefore, that followed after, read what was written, and escaped the danger. This done, they sang as follows:

"Out of the way we went, and then we found
What 'twas to tread upon forbidden ground:
And let them that come after have a care,
Lest heedlessness makes them as we to fare;
Lest they, for trespassing, his prisoners are,
Whose castle's Doubting, and whose name's Despair."

# 31

# Mountains &
# Shepherds

THEY WENT then till they came to the Delectable
Mountains, which mountains belong to the Lord
of that hill of which we have spoken before. So they
went up to the mountains, to behold the gardens and
orchards, the vineyards and fountains of water; where
also they drank and washed themselves, and did freely
eat of the vineyards. Now, there were on the tops of
these mountains shepherds feeding their flocks, and
they stood by the highway-side. The pilgrims, therefore, went to them, and leaning upon their staffs, (as is
common with weary pilgrims when they stand to talk
with any by the way,) they asked, Whose Delectable
Mountains are these; and whose be the sheep that feed
upon them?

> THE SHEPHERDS: These mountains are
> Emmanuel's land, and they are within sight of
> his city; and the sheep also are his, and he laid
> down his life for them.                    *John 10:11, 15*

> CHRISTIAN: Is this the way to the Celestial
> City?

> THE SHEPHERDS: You are just in your way.

> CHRISTIAN: How far is it thither?

THE SHEPHERDS: Too far for any but those who shall get thither indeed.

CHRISTIAN: Is the way safe or dangerous?

THE SHEPHERDS: Safe for those for whom it is to be safe; but transgressors shall fall therein.

*Hosea 14:9*

CHRISTIAN: Is there in this place any relief for pilgrims that are weary and faint in the way?

THE SHEPHERDS: The Lord of these mountains hath given us a charge not to be forgetful to entertain strangers; therefore the good of the place is before you.

*Hebrews 13:2*

I saw also in my dream, that when the shepherds perceived that they were wayfaring men, they also put questions to them, (to which they made answer as in other places,) as, Whence came you? and, How got you into the way? and, By what means have you so persevered therein? for but few of them that begin to come hither, do show their face on these mountains. But when the shepherds heard their answers, being pleased therewith, they looked very lovingly upon them, and said, Welcome to the Delectable Mountains.

The shepherds, I say, whose names were Knowledge, Experience, Watchful, and Sincere, took them by the hand, and had them to their tents, and made them partake of that which was ready at present. They said moreover, We would that you should stay here a while, to be acquainted with us, and yet more to solace yourselves with the good of these Delectable Mountains. Then they told them that they were content to stay. So they went to their rest that night, because it was very late.

Then I saw in my dream, that in the morning the shepherds called up Christian and Hopeful to walk with them upon the mountains. So they went forth with them, and walked a while, having a pleasant prospect on every side. Then said the shepherds one to another, Shall we show these pilgrims some wonders? So when they had concluded to do it, they had them first to the top of a hill called Error, which was very steep on the farthest side, and bid them look down to the bottom. So Christian and Hopeful looked down, and saw at the bottom several men dashed all to pieces by a fall that they had had from the top. Then said Christian, What meaneth this? The shepherds answered, Have you not heard of them that were made to err, by hearkening to Hymenius and Philetus, as concerning the faith of the resurrection of the body? They answered, Yes. Then said the shepherds, Those that you see lie dashed in pieces at the bottom of this mountain are they; and they have continued to this day unburied, as you see, for an example to others to take heed how they clamber too high, or how they come too near the brink of this mountain.

*2 Timothy 2:17–18*

Then I saw that they had them to the top of another mountain, and the name of that is Caution, and bid them look afar off; which, when they did, they perceived, as they thought, several men walking up and down among the tombs that were there; and they perceived that the men were blind, because they stumbled sometimes upon the tombs, and because they could not get out from among them. Then said Christian, What means this?

The shepherds then answered, Did you not see, a little below these mountains, a stile that led into a meadow, on the left hand of this way? They answered, Yes. Then said the shepherds, From that stile there goes a path that leads directly to Doubting Castle, which is kept by Giant Despair; and these men (pointing to them among the tombs) came once on pilgrimage, as you do now, even until they came to that same stile. And because the right way was rough in that place, they chose to go out of it into that meadow, and there were taken by Giant Despair, and cast into Doubting Castle; where after they had a while been kept in the dungeon, he at last did put out their eyes, and led them among those tombs, where he has left them to wander to this very day, that the saying of the wise man might be fulfilled, "He that wandereth out of the way of understanding shall remain in the congregation of the dead." Then Christian and Hopeful looked upon one another, with tears gushing

*Proverbs 21:16*

out, but yet said nothing to the shepherds.

Then I saw in my dream, that the shepherds had them to another place in a bottom, where was a door on the side of a hill; and they opened the door, and bid them look in. They looked in, therefore, and saw that within it was very dark and smoky; they also thought that they heard there a rumbling noise, as of fire, and a cry of some tormented, and that they smelt the scent of brimstone. Then said Christian, What means this? The shepherds told them, This is a by-way to hell, a way that hypocrites go in at; namely, such as sell their birthright, with Esau; such as sell their Master, with Judas; such as blaspheme the Gospel, with Alexander; and that lie and dissemble, with Ananias and Sapphira his wife.

Then said Hopeful to the shepherds, I perceive that these had on them, even every one, a show of pilgrimage, as we have now; had they not?

THE SHEPHERDS: Yes, and held it a long time, too.

HOPEFUL: How far might they go on in pilgrimage in their day, since they, notwithstanding, were miserably cast away?

THE SHEPHERDS: Some farther, and some not so far as these mountains.

Then said the pilgrims one to the other, We had need to cry to the Strong for strength.

THE SHEPHERDS: Aye, and you will have need to use it, when you have it, too.

By this time the pilgrims had a desire to go forward, and the shepherds a desire they should; so they walked together towards the end of the mountains. Then said the shepherds one to another, Let us here show the pilgrims the gates of the Celestial City, if they have skill to look through our perspective glass. The pilgrims lovingly accepted the motion: so they had them to the top of a high hill, called Clear, and gave them the glass to look.

Then they tried to look; but the remembrance of that last thing that the shepherds had shown them made their hands shake, by means of which impediment they could not look steadily through the glass; yet they thought they saw something like the gate, and also some of the glory of the place. Then they went away, and sang,

"Thus by the shepherds secrets are reveal'd,
Which from all other men are kept concealed:
Come to the shepherds then, if you would see
Things deep, things hid, and that mysterious be."

When they were about to depart, one of the shepherds gave them a note of the way. Another of them bid them beware of the Flatterer. The third bid them take heed that they slept not upon Enchanted Ground. And the fourth bid them God speed. So I awoke from my dream.

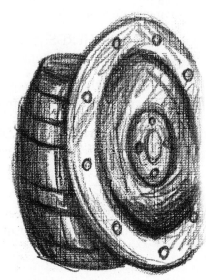

# 32

# IGNORANCE,
# TURN-AWAY
# & LITTLE-FAITH

A ND I slept, and dreamed again, and saw the same two pilgrims going down the mountains along the highway towards the city. Now, a little below these mountains, on the left hand, lieth the country of Conceit, from which country there comes into the way in which the pilgrims walked, a little crooked lane. Here, therefore, they met with a very brisk lad that came out of that country, and his name was Ignorance. So Christian asked him from what parts he came, and whither he was going.

IGNORANCE: Sir, I was born in the country that lieth off there, a little on the left hand, and I am going to the Celestial City.

CHRISTIAN: But how do you think to get in at the gate, for you may find some difficulty there?

IGNORANCE: As other good people do, said he.

CHRISTIAN: But what have you to show at that gate, that the gate should be opened to you?

IGNORANCE: I know my Lord's will, and have

been a good liver; I pay every man his own; I pray, fast, pay tithes, and give alms, and have left my country for whither I am going.

CHRISTIAN: But thou camest not in at the wicket-gate, that is at the head of this way; thou camest in hither through that same crooked lane, and therefore I fear, however thou mayest think of thyself, when the reckoning-day shall come, thou wilt have laid to thy charge, that thou art a thief and a robber, instead of getting admittance into the city.

IGNORANCE: Gentlemen, ye be utter strangers to me; I know you not: be content to follow the religion of your country, and I will follow the religion of mine. I hope all will be well. And as for the gate that you talk of, all the world knows that is a great way off of our country. I cannot think that any man in all our parts doth so much as know the way to it; nor need they matter whether they do or no, since we have, as you see, a fine, pleasant, green lane, that comes down from our country, the next way into the way.

When Christian saw that the man was wise in his own conceit, he said to Hopeful whisperingly, "There is *Proverbs 26:12* more hope of a fool than of him." And said, moreover, "When he that is a fool walketh by the way, his wisdom *Ecclesiastes 10:3* faileth him, and he saith to every one that he is a fool. What, shall we talk farther with him, or outgo him at present, and so leave him to think of what he hath heard already, and then stop again for him afterwards, and see if by degrees we can do any good to him? Then said Hopeful,

"Let Ignorance a little while now muse

On what is said, and let him not refuse
Good counsel to embrace, lest he remain
Still ignorant of what's the chiefest gain.
God saith, those that no understanding have,
(Although he made them,) them he will not save."

HOPEFUL: He further added, It is not good, I think, to say so to him all at once; let us pass him by, if you will, and talk to him anon, even as he is able to bear it.

So they both went on, and Ignorance he came after. Now, when they had passed him a little way, they entered into a very dark lane, where they met a man whom seven devils had bound with seven strong cords, and were carrying him back to the door that they saw on the side of the hill. Now good Christian began to trem-

*Matthew 12:45*
*Proverbs 5:22*

ble, and so did Hopeful, his companion; yet, as the devils led away the man, Christian looked to see if he knew him; and he thought it might be one Turn-away, that dwelt in the town of Apostacy. But he did not perfectly see his face, for he did hang his head like a thief that is found; but being gone past, Hopeful looked after him, and espied on his back a paper with this inscription, "Wanton professor, and damnable apostate."

Then said Christian to his fellow, Now I call to remembrance that which was told me of a thing that happened to a good man hereabout. The name of the man was Little-Faith; but a good man, and he dwelt in the town of Sincere. The thing was this. At the entering in at this passage, there comes down from Broadway-gate, a lane, called Dead-Man's lane; so called because of the murders that are commonly done there; and this Little-Faith going on pilgrimage, as we do now, chanced to sit down there and sleep. Now there happened at that time to come down the lane from Broadway-gate, three sturdy rogues, and their names were Faint-Heart, Mistrust, and Guilt, three brothers; and they, espying Little-Faith where he was, came galloping up with speed. Now the good man was just awaked from his sleep, and was getting up to go on his journey. So they came up all to him, and with threatening language bid him stand. At this, Little-Faith looked as white as a sheet, and had neither power to fight nor fly. Then said Faint-Heart, Deliver thy purse; but he making no haste to do it, (for he was loth to lose his money,) Mistrust ran up to him, and thrusting his hand into his pocket, pulled out thence a bag of silver. Then he cried out, Thieves, thieves! With that, Guilt, with a great club that was in his hand, struck Little-Faith on the head, and with that blow felled him flat to the ground, where he lay bleeding as one that would bleed to death. All this while the thieves stood by. But at last, they hearing that some were upon the road, and fearing lest it should be one Great-Grace, that dwells in the town of Good-Confidence, they betook themselves to their heels, and left this good man to shift for himself. Now, after a while, Little-Faith came to himself, and getting up, made shift to scramble on his way. This was the story.

HOPEFUL: But did they take from him all that ever he had?

CHRISTIAN: No; the place where his jewels were they never ransacked; so those he kept still. But, as I was told, the good man was much afflicted for his loss; for the thieves got most of his spending-money. That which they got not, as I said, were jewels; also, he had a little odd money left, but scarce enough to bring him to his journey's end. Nay, (if I was not misinformed,) he was forced to beg as he went, to keep himself alive, for his jewels he might not sell; but beg and do what he could, he went, as we say, with many a hungry belly the most part of the rest of the way.

*1 Peter 4:18*

HOPEFUL: But is it not a wonder they got not from him his certificate, by which he was to receive his admittance at the Celestial Gate?

CHRISTIAN: It is a wonder; but they got not that, though they missed it not through any good cunning of his; for he, being dismayed by their coming upon him, had neither power nor skill to hide any thing; so it was more by good providence than by his endeavor that they missed of that good thing.

*2 Timothy 1:12–14*
*2 Peter 2:9*

# 33

# CHRISTIAN &
# HOPEFUL, GREAT-
# GRACE

HOPEFUL: But it must needs be a comfort to him they got not this jewel from him.

CHRISTIAN: It might have been great comfort to him, had he used it as he should; but they that told me the story said that he made but little use of it all the rest of the way, and that because of the dismay that he had in their taking away his money. Indeed, he forgot it a great part of the rest of his journey; and besides, when at any time it came into his mind, and he began to be comforted therewith, then would fresh thoughts of his loss come again upon him, and these thoughts would swallow up all.

HOPEFUL: Alas, poor man, this could not but be a great grief to him.

CHRISTIAN: Grief? Aye, a grief indeed! Would it not have been so to any of us, had we been used as he, to be robbed and wounded too, and that in a strange place, as he was? It is a wonder he did not die with grief, poor heart. I was told that he scattered almost all the rest of the way with nothing but doleful and bitter complaints; telling, also, to all that overtook him, or that he overtook in the way as he went, where he was robbed, and how; who they were that did it, and what he had lost; how he was wounded, and that he hardly escaped with life.

HOPEFUL: But it is a wonder that his necessity did not put him upon selling or pawning some of his jewels, that he might have wherewith to relieve himself in his journey.

CHRISTIAN: Thou talkest like one upon whose head is the shell to this very day. For what should he pawn them? or to whom should he sell them? In all that country where he was robbed, his jewels were not accounted of; nor did he want that relief which could from thence be administered to him. Besides, had his jewels been missing at the gate of the Celestial City, he had (and that he knew well enough) been excluded from an inheritance there, and that would have been worse to him than the appearance and villany of ten thousand thieves.

HOPEFUL: Why art thou so tart, my brother? Esau sold his birthright, and that for a mess of pottage, and that birthright was his greatest jewel: and if he, why might not Little-Faith do so too?

*Hebrews 12:16*

CHRISTIAN: Esau did sell his birthright indeed, and so do many besides, and by so doing exclude themselves from the chief blessing, as also that caitiff did; but you must put a difference betwixt Esau and Little-Faith, and also betwixt their estates. Esau's birthright was typical; but Little-Faith's jewels were not so. Esau's belly was his god; but Little-Faith's belly was not so. Esau's want lay in his fleshy appetite; Little-Faith's did not so. Besides, Esau could see no further than to the fulfilling of his lusts: For I am at the point to die, said he: and what good will this birthright do me? But Little-Faith, though it was his lot to have but a little faith, was by his little faith kept from such extravagances, and made to see and prize his jewels more than to sell them, as Esau did his birthright. You read not any where that Esau had faith, no, not so much as a little; therefore no marvel, where the flesh only bears sway, (as it will in that man where no faith is to resist,) if he sells his birthright and his soul and all, and that to the devil of hell; for it is with such as it is with the ass, who in her occasion cannot be turned away: when their minds are set upon their lusts, they will have them, whatever they cost. But Little-Faith was of another temper; his mind was on things divine; his livelihood was upon things that were spiritual, and from above: therefore, to what end should he that is of such a temper sell his jewels (had there been any that would have bought them) to fill his mind with empty things? Will a man give a penny to fill his belly with hay? or can you persuade the turtle-dove to live upon carrion, like the crow? Though faithless ones can, for carnal lusts, pawn, or mortgage, or sell what they have, and themselves outright to boot; yet they that have faith, saving faith, though but a little of it, cannot do so. Here, therefore, my brother, is thy mistake.

*Genesis 25:32*

*Jeremiah 2:24*

HOPEFUL: I acknowledge it; but yet your severe reflection had almost made me angry.

CHRISTIAN: Why, I did but compare thee to

some of the birds that are of the brisker sort, who will run to and fro in untrodden paths with the shell upon their heads: but pass by that, and consider the matter under debate, and all shall be well betwixt thee and me.

HOPEFUL: But, Christian, these three fellows, I am persuaded in my heart, are but a company of cowards: would they have run else, think you, as they did, at the noise of one that was coming on the road? Why did not Little-Faith pluck up a greater heart? He might, methinks, have stood one brush with them, and have yielded when there had been no remedy.

CHRISTIAN: That they are cowards, many have said, but few have found it so in the time of trial. As for a great heart, Little-Faith had none; and I perceive by thee, my brother, hadst thou been the man concerned, thou art but for a brush, and then to yield. And verily, since this is the height of thy stomach now they are at a distance from us, should they appear to thee as they did to him, they might put thee to second thoughts.

But consider again, that they are but journeymen thieves; They serve under the king of the bottomless pit, who, if need be, will come to their aid himself, and his voice is as the roaring of a lion. I myself have been engaged as this Little-Faith was, and I found it a terrible thing. These three villains set upon me, and I beginning like a Christian to resist, they gave but a call, and in came their master. I would, as the saying is, have given my life for a penny, but that, as God would have it, I was clothed with armor of proof. Aye, and yet, though I was so harnessed, I found it hard work to

*1 Peter 5:8*

quit myself like a man: no man can tell what in that combat attends us, but he that hath been in the battle himself.

HOPEFUL: Well, but they ran, you see, when they did but suppose that one Great-Grace was in the way.

CHRISTIAN: True, they have often fled, both they and their master, when Great-Grace hath but appeared; and no marvel, for he is the King's champion. But I trow you will put some difference between Little-Faith and the King's champion. All the King's subjects are not his champions; nor can they, when tried, do such feats of war as he. Is it meet to think that a little child should handle Goliath as David did? or that there should be the strength of an ox in a wren? Some are strong, some are weak; some have great faith, some have little: this man was one of the weak, and therefore he went to the wall.

HOPEFUL: I would it had been Great-Grace, for their sakes.

CHRISTIAN: If it had been he, he might have had his hands full: for I must tell you, that though Great-Grace is excellent good at his weapons, and has, and can, so long as he keeps them at sword's point, do well enough with them; yet if they get within him, even Faint-Heart, Mistrust, or the other, it shall go hard but they will throw up his heels. And when a man is down, you know, what can he do?

Whoso looks well upon Great-Grace's face, will see those scars and cuts there that shall easily give demonstration of what I say. Yea, once I

Psalm 88

heard that he should say, (and that when he was in the combat,) We despaired even of life. How did these sturdy rogues and their fellows make David groan, mourn, and roar! Yea, Heman, and Hezekiah too, though champions in their days, were forced to bestir them when by these assaulted; and yet, notwithstanding, they had their coats soundly brushed by them. Peter, upon a time, would go try what he could do; but though some do say of him that he is the prince of the apostles, they handled him so that they made him at last afraid of a sorry girl.

Besides, their king is at their whistle; he is never out of hearing; and if at any time they be put to the worst, he, if possible, comes in to help them; and of him it is said, "The sword of him that layeth at him cannot hold; the spear, the dart, nor the habergeon. He esteemeth iron as straw, and brass as rotten wood. The arrow cannot make him fly; sling-stones are turned with him into stubble. Darts are counted as stubble; he Job 41:26–29 laugheth at the shaking of a spear." What can a man do in this case? It is true, if a man could at every turn have Job's horse, and had skill and courage to ride him, he might do notable things. "For his neck is clothed with thunder. He will not be afraid as a grasshopper: the glory of his nostrils is terrible. He paweth in the valley, and rejoiceth in his strength; he goeth on to meet the armed men. He mocketh at fear, and is not affrighted; neither turneth he back from the sword. The quiver rattleth against him, the glittering spear and the shield. He swalloweth the ground with fierceness and rage; neither believeth he that it is the sound of the trumpet.

He saith among the trumpets, Ha, ha! and he smelleth the battle afar off, the thunder of the captains, and the shoutings."

*Job 39:19–25*

But for such footmen as thee and I are, let us never desire to meet with an enemy, nor vaunt as if we could do better, when we hear of others that have been foiled, nor be tickled at the thoughts of our own manhood; for such commonly come by the worst when tried. Witness Peter, of whom I made mention before: he would swagger, aye, he would; he would, as his vain mind prompted him to say, do better and stand more for his Master than all men: but who so foiled and run down by those villains as he?

When, therefore, we hear that such robberies are done on the King's highway, two things become us to do.

To go out harnessed, and be sure to take a shield with us: for it was for want of that, that he who laid so lustily at Leviathan could not make him yield; for, indeed, if that be wanting, he fears us not at all. Therefore, he that had skill hath said, "Above all, take the shield of faith, wherewith ye shall be able to quench all the fiery darts of the wicked."

*Ephesians 6:16*

It is good, also, that we desire of the King a convoy, yea, that he will go with us himself. This made David rejoice when in the Valley of the Shadow of Death; and Moses was rather for dying where he stood, than to go one step without his God.

*Exodus 33:15*

O, my brother, if he will but go along with us, what need we be afraid of ten thousands that

Psalm 3:5–8;
27:1–3
Isaiah 10:4

shall set themselves against us? But without him, the proud helpers fall under the slain.

I, for my part, have been in the fray before now; and though (through the goodness of Him that is best) I am, as you see, alive, yet I cannot boast of any manhood. Glad shall I be if I meet with no more such brunts; though I fear we are not got beyond all danger. However, since the lion and the bear have not as yet devoured me, I hope God will also deliver us from the next un-circumcised Philistine. Then sang Christian,

"Poor Little-Faith! hast been among the thieves?
Wast robb'd? Remember this, whoso believes,
And get more faith; then shall you victors be
Over ten thousand—else scarce over three."

# 34

# FLATTERER & SHINING ONE, ATHEIST

S O THEY went on, and Ignorance followed. They went then till they came at a place where they saw a way put itself into their way, and seemed withal to lie as strait as the way which they should go; and here they knew not which of the two to take, for both seemed strait before them: therefore here they stood still to consider. And as they were thinking about the way, behold a man black of flesh, but covered with a very light robe, come to them, and asked them why they stood there. They answered, they were going to the Celestial City, but knew not which of these ways to take. "Follow me," said the man, "it is thither that I am going." So they followed him in the way that but now came into the road, which by degrees turned, and turned them so far from the city that they desired to go to, that in a little time their faces were turned away from it; yet they follow him. But by and by, before they were aware, he led them both within the compass of a net, in which they were both so entangled that they knew not what to do; and with that the white robe fell off the black man's back. Then they saw where they were. Wherefore there they lay crying some time, for they could not get themselves out.

CHRISTIAN: Then said Christian to his fellow, Now do I see myself in an error. Did not the

*Proverbs 29:5*

shepherds bid us beware of the Flatterer? As is the saying of the wise man, so we have found it this day: "A man that flattereth his neighbor, spreadeth a net for his feet."

HOPEFUL: They also gave us a note of directions about the way, for our more sure finding thereof; but therein we have also forgotten to read, and have not kept ourselves from the paths of the destroyer. Here David was wiser than we; for saith he, "Concerning the works of men, by the word of thy lips I have kept me from the paths of the Destroyer." Thus they lay bewailing themselves in the net. At last they espied a Shining One coming towards them with a whip of small cords in his hand. When he was come to the place where they were, he asked them whence they came, and what they did there. They told him that they were poor pilgrims going to Zion, but were led out of their way by a black man clothed in white, who bid us, said they, follow him, for he was going thither too. Then said he with the whip, It is Flatterer, a false apostle, that hath transformed himself into an angel of light. So he rent the net, and let the men out. Then said he to them, Follow me, that I may set you in your way again. So he led them back to the way which they had left to follow the Flatterer. Then he asked them, saying, Where did you lie the last night? They said, With the shepherds upon the Delectable Mountains. He asked them then if they had not of the shepherds a note of direction for the way. They answered, Yes. But did you not, said he, when you were at a stand, pluck out and read your note? They answered, No. He asked them, Why? They said they forgot. He asked, moreover, if the shepherds did not bid them beware of the Flatterer. They answered, Yes; but we did not imagine, said they, that this fine-spoken man had been he.

Then I saw in my dream, that he commanded them to lie down; which when they did, he chastised them sore, to teach them the good way wherein they should

*Psalm 17:4*

*Daniel 11:32*
*2 Corinthians 11:13–14*

*Romans 16:17–18*

Deuteronomy 25:2
2 Chronicles 6:27

Revelation 3:19

walk; and as he chastised them, he said, "As many as I love, I rebuke and chasten; be zealous, therefore, and repent." This done, he bids them to go on their way, and take good heed to the other directions of the shepherds. So they thanked him for all his kindness, and went softly along the right way, singing,

> "Come hither, you that walk along the way,
> See how the pilgrims fare that go astray:
> They catched are in an entangling net,
> Cause they good counsel lightly did forget:
> 'Tis true, they rescued were; but yet, you see,
> They're scouged to boot; let this your caution be."

Now, after awhile, they perceived afar off, one coming softly, and alone, all along the highway, to meet them. Then said Christian to his fellow, Yonder is a man with his back towards Zion, and he is coming to meet us.

HOPEFUL: I see him; let us take heed to ourselves now, lest he should prove a Flatterer also. So he drew nearer and nearer, and at last came up to them. His name was Atheist, and he asked them whither they were going.

CHRISTIAN: We are going to Mount Zion.

Then Atheist fell into a very great laughter.

CHRISTIAN: What's the meaning of your laughter?

ATHEIST: I laugh to see what ignorant persons you are, to take upon you so tedious a journey, and yet are like to have nothing but your travel for your pains.

CHRISTIAN: Why, man, do you think we shall not be received?

ATHEIST: Received! There is not such a place as you dream of in all this world.

CHRISTIAN: But there is in the world to come.

ATHEIST: When I was at home in mine own country I heard as you now affirm, and from that hearing went out to see, and have been seeking this city these twenty years, but find no more of it than I did the first day I set out.

*Ecclesiastes 10:15*
*Jeremiah 17:15*

CHRISTIAN: We have both heard, and believe, that there is such a place to be found.

ATHEIST: Had not I, when at home, believed, I had not come thus far to seek; but finding none, (and yet I should, had there been such a place to be found, for I have gone to seek it farther than you,) I am going back again, and will seek to refresh myself with the things that I then cast away for hopes of that which I now see is not.

CHRISTIAN: Then said Christian to Hopeful his companion, Is it true which this man hath said?

HOPEFUL: Take heed, he is one of the Flatterers. Remember what it cost us once already for our hearkening to such kind of fellows. What! No Mount Zion? Did we not see from the Delectable Mountains the gate of the city? Also, are we not now to walk by faith?

*2 Corinthians 5:7*

Let us go on, lest the man with the whip overtake us again. You should have taught me that lesson, which I will sound you in the ears withal: "Cease, my son, to hear the instruction that causeth to err from the words of knowledge." I say, my brother, cease to hear him, and let us

*Proverbs 19:27*

believe to the saving of the soul.

CHRISTIAN: My brother, I did not put the question to thee, for that I doubted of the truth of our belief myself, but to prove thee, and to fetch from thee a fruit of the honesty of thy heart. As for this man, I know that he is blinded by the God of this world. Let thee and me go on, knowing that we have belief of the truth; and no lie is of the truth.

*1 John 5:21*

HOPEFUL: Now do I rejoice in hope of the glory of God. So they turned away from the man; and he, laughing at them, went his way.

# 35

# ENCHANTED GROUNDS, HOPEFUL'S TESTIMONY

I THEN SAW in my dream that they went on until they came into a certain country whose air naturally tended to make one drowsy, if he came a stranger into it. And here Hopeful began to be very dull, and heavy to sleep: wherefore he said unto Christian, I do now begin to grow so drowsy that I can scarcely hold open mine eyes; let us lie down here, and take one nap.

CHRISTIAN: By no means, said the other; lest, sleeping, we never awake more.

HOPEFUL: Why, my brother? Sleep is sweet to the laboring man; we may be refreshed, if we take a nap.

CHRISTIAN: Do you not remember that one of the shepherds bid us beware of the Enchanted Ground? He meant by that, that we should beware of sleeping; wherefore "let us not sleep, as do others; but let us watch and be sober."

*1 Thessalonians 5:6*

HOPEFUL: I acknowledge myself in a fault; and had I been here alone, I had by sleeping run the danger of death. I see it is true that the wise man

*Ecclesiastes 4:9*

saith, "Two are better than one." Hitherto hath thy company been my mercy; and thou shalt have a good reward for thy labor.

CHRISTIAN: Now, then, said Christian, to prevent drowsiness in this place, let us fall into good discourse.

HOPEFUL: With all my heart, said the other.

CHRISTIAN: Where shall we begin?

HOPEFUL: Where God began with us. But do you begin, if you please.

CHRISTIAN: I will sing you first this song:

"When saints do sleepy grow, let them come hither,
And hear how these two pilgrims talk together;
Yea, let them learn of them in any wise,
Thus to keep ope their drowsy, slumb'ring eyes.
Saints' fellowship, if it be managed well,
Keeps them awake, and that in spite of hell."

Then Christian began, and said, I will ask you a question. How came you to think at first of doing what you do now?

HOPEFUL: Do you mean, how came I at first to look after the good of my soul?

CHRISTIAN: Yes, that is my meaning.

HOPEFUL: I continued a great while in the delight of those things which were seen and sold at our fair; things which I believe now would have, had I continued in them still, drowned me in perdition and destruction.

CHRISTIAN: What things were they?

HOPEFUL: All the treasures and riches of the world. Also I delighted much in rioting, reveling, drinking, swearing, lying, uncleanness, Sabbath-breaking, and what not, that tended to destroy the soul. But I found at last, by hearing and considering of things that are divine, which, indeed, I heard of you, as also of beloved Faithful, that was put to death for his faith and good living in Vanity Fair, that the end of these things is death,   and    *Romans 6:21–23*

*Ephesians 5:6*
that for these things' sake, the wrath of God cometh upon the children of disobedience.

CHRISTIAN: And did you presently fall under the power of this conviction?

HOPEFUL: No, I was not willing presently to know the evil of sin, nor the damnation that follows upon the commission of it; but endeavored, when my mind at first began to be shaken with the word, to shut mine eyes against the light thereof.

CHRISTIAN: But what was the cause of your carrying of it thus to the first workings of God's blessed Spirit upon you?

HOPEFUL: The causes were,

1. I was ignorant that this was the work of God upon me. I never thought that by awakenings for sin, God at first begins the conversion of a sinner.

2. Sin was yet very sweet to my flesh, and I was loth to leave it.

3. I could not tell how to part with mine old companions, their presence and actions were so desirable unto me.

4. The hours in which convictions were upon me, were such troublesome and such heart-affrighting hours, that I could not bear, no not so much as the remembrance of them upon my heart.

CHRISTIAN: Then, as it seems, sometimes you got rid of your trouble?

HOPEFUL: Yes, verily, but it would come into

my mind again; and then I should be as bad, nay, worse than I was before.

CHRISTIAN: Why, what was it that brought your sins to mind again?

HOPEFUL: Many things; as,

1. If I did but meet a good man in the streets; or,

2. If I have heard any read in the Bible; or,

3. If mine head did begin to ache; or,

4. If I were told that some of my neighbors were sick; or,

5. If I heard the bell toll for some that were dead; or,

6. If I thought of dying myself; or,

7. If I heard that sudden death happened to others.

8. But especially when I thought of myself, that I must quickly come to judgment.

CHRISTIAN: And could you at any time, with ease, get off the guilt of sin, when by any of these ways it came upon you?

HOPEFUL: No, not I; for then they got faster hold of my conscience; and then, if I did but think of going back to sin, (though my mind was turned against it,) it would be double torment to me.

CHRISTIAN: And how did you do then?

HOPEFUL: I thought I must endeavor to mend

my life; for else, thought I, I am sure to be damned.

CHRISTIAN: And did you endeavor to mend?

HOPEFUL: Yes, and fled from, not only my sins, but sinful company too, and betook me to religious duties, as praying, reading, weeping for sin, speaking truth to my neighbors, etc. These things did I, with many others, too much here to relate.

CHRISTIAN: And did you think yourself well then?

HOPEFUL: Yes, for a while; but at the last my trouble came tumbling upon me again, and that over the neck of all my reformations.

CHRISTIAN: How came that about, since you were now reformed?

*Isaiah 64:6*

*Galatians 2:16*

*Luke 17:10*

HOPEFUL: There were several things brought it upon me, especially such sayings as these: "All our righteousnesses are as filthy rags." "By the works of the law shall no flesh be justified." "When ye have done all these things, say, We are unprofitable," with many more such like. From whence I began to reason with myself thus: If all my righteousnesses are as filthy rags; if by the deeds of the law no man can be justified; and if, when we have done all, we are yet unprofitable, then is it but a folly to think of heaven by the law. I farther thought thus: If a man runs a hundred pounds into the shopkeeper's debt, and after that shall pay for all that he shall fetch; yet if his old debt stands still in the book uncrossed, the shopkeeper may sue him for it, and cast him into prison, till he shall pay the debt.

CHRISTIAN: Well, and how did you apply this to yourself?

HOPEFUL: Why, I thought thus with myself: I have by my sins run a great way into God's book, and my now reforming will not pay off that score; therefore I should think still, under all my present amendments, But how shall I be freed from that damnation that I brought myself in danger of by my former transgressions?

CHRISTIAN: A very good application: but pray go on.

HOPEFUL: Another thing that hath troubled me ever since my late amendments, is, that if I look narrowly into the best of what I do now, I still see sin, new sin, mixing itself with the best of that I do; so that now I am forced to conclude, that notwithstanding my former fond conceits of myself and duties, I have committed sin enough in one day to send me to hell, though my former life had been faultless.

CHRISTIAN: And what did you do then?

HOPEFUL: Do! I could not tell what to do, until I broke my mind to Faithful; for he and I were well acquainted. And he told me, that unless I could obtain the righteousness of a man that never had sinned, neither mine own, nor all the righteousness of the world, could save me.

CHRISTIAN: And did you think he spake true?

HOPEFUL: Had he told me so when I was pleased and satisfied with my own amendments, I had called him fool for his pains; but now, since I see my own infirmity, and the sin which cleaves to my best performance, I have been forced to be of his opinion.

CHRISTIAN: But did you think, when at first he suggested it to you, that there was such a man to be found, of whom it might justly be said, that he never committed sin?

HOPEFUL: I must confess the words at first sounded strangely; but after a little more talk and company with him, I had full conviction about it.

CHRISTIAN: And did you ask him what man this was, and how you must be justified by him?

*Hebrews 10:12–21*

*Romans 4:5*
*Colossians 1:14*
*1 Peter 1:19*

HOPEFUL: Yes, and he told me it was the Lord Jesus, that dwelleth on the right hand of the Most High. And thus, said he, you must be justified by him, even by trusting to what he hath done by himself in the days of his flesh, and suffered when he did hang on the tree. I asked him further, how that man's righteousness could be of that efficacy, to justify another before God. And he told me he was the mighty God, and did what he did, and died the death also, not for himself, but for me; to whom his doings, and the worthiness of them, should be imputed, if I believed on him.

CHRISTIAN: And what did you do then?

HOPEFUL: I made my objections against my believing, for that I thought he was not willing to save me.

CHRISTIAN: And what said Faithful to you then?

HOPEFUL: He bid me go to him and see. Then

I said it was presumption. He said, No; for I was invited to come. Then he gave me a book of Jesus' inditing, to encourage me the more freely to come; and he said concerning that book, that every jot and tittle thereof stood firmer than heaven and earth. Then I asked him what I must do when I came; and he told me I must entreat upon my knees, with all my heart and soul, the Father to reveal him to me. Then I asked him further, how I must make my supplications to him; and he said, Go, and thou shalt find him upon a mercy-seat, where he sits all the year long to give pardon and forgiveness to them that come. I told him, that I knew not what to say when I came; and he bid say to this effect: God be merciful to me a sinner, and make me to know and believe in Jesus Christ; for I see, that if his righteousness had not been, or I have not faith in that righteousness, I am utterly cast away. Lord, I have heard that thou art a merciful God, and hast ordained that thy Son Jesus Christ should be the Saviour of the world; and moreover, that thou art willing to bestow him upon such a poor sinner as I am-and I am a sinner indeed. Lord, take therefore this opportunity, and magnify thy grace in the salvation of my soul, through thy Son Jesus Christ. Amen.

*Matthew 11:28*

*Matthew 24:35*

*Psalm 95:6*
*Daniel 6:10*

*Jeremiah 29:12–13*

*Exodus 25:22*
*Leviticus 16:2*
*Numbers 7:89*
*Hebrews 4:16*

CHRISTIAN: And did you do as you were bidden?

HOPEFUL: Yes, over, and over, and over.

CHRISTIAN: And did the Father reveal the Son to you?

HOPEFUL: Not at the first, nor second, nor third, nor fourth, nor fifth, no, nor at the sixth time neither.

CHRISTIAN: What did you do then?

HOPEFUL: What? why I could not tell what to do.

CHRISTIAN: Had you not thoughts of leaving off praying?

HOPEFUL: Yes; an hundred times twice told.

CHRISTIAN: And what was the reason you did not?

HOPEFUL: I believed that it was true which hath been told me, to wit, that without the righteousness of this Christ, all the world could not save me; and therefore, thought I with myself, if I leave off, I die, and I can but die at the throne of grace. And withal this came into my mind, "If it tarry, wait for it; because it will surely come, and will not tarry." . So I continued praying until the Father showed me his Son.

*Habakkuk 2:3*

CHRISTIAN: And how was he revealed unto you?

HOPEFUL: I did not see him with my bodily eyes, but with the eyes of my understanding, and thus it was. One day I was very sad, I think sadder than at any one time in my life; and this sadness was through a fresh sight of the greatness and vileness of my sins. And as I was then looking for nothing but hell, and the everlasting damnation of my soul, suddenly, as I thought, I saw the Lord Jesus looking down from heaven upon me, and saying, "Believe on the Lord Jesus Christ, and thou shalt be saved."

*Ephesians 1:18–19*

*Acts 16:31*

But I replied, Lord, I am a great, a very great sinner: and he answered, "My grace is sufficient for thee." Then I said, But, Lord, what is believing? And then I saw from that saying, "He that co-

*2 Corinthians 12:9*

meth to me shall never hunger, and he that believeth on me shall never thirst," that believing
and coming was all one; and that he that came,
that is, that ran out in his heart and affections
after salvation by Christ, he indeed believed in
Christ. Then the water stood in mine eyes, and
I asked further, But, Lord, may such a great sinner as I am be indeed accepted of thee, and be
saved by thee? And I heard him say, "And him
that cometh to me, I will in no wise cast out."
Then I said, But how, Lord, must I consider of
thee in my coming to thee, that my faith may be
placed aright upon thee? Then he said, "Christ
Jesus came into the world to save sinners." He
is the end of the law for righteousness to every
one that believes. He died for our sins, and rose
again for our justification. He loved us, and
washed us from our sins in his own blood. He is
the Mediator between God and us. He ever
liveth to make intercession for us. From all
which I gathered, that I must look for righteousness in his person, and for satisfaction for my
sins by his blood: that what he did in obedience
to his Father's law, and in submitting to the pen-
alty thereof, was not for himself, but for him
that will accept it for his salvation, and be
thankful. And now was my heart full of joy,
mine eyes full of tears, and mine affections running over with love to the name, people, and
ways of Jesus Christ.

*John 6:35*

*John 6:37*

*1 Timothy 1:15*

*Romans 10:4*
*Romans 4:25*
*Revelation 1:5*

*1 Timothy 2:5*
*Hebrews 7:25*

CHRISTIAN: This was a revelation of Christ to
your soul indeed. But tell me particularly what
effect this had upon your spirit.

HOPEFUL: It made me see that all the world,
notwithstanding all the righteousness thereof,

is in a state of condemnation. It made me see that God the Father, though he be just, can justly justify the coming sinner. It made me greatly ashamed of the vileness of my former life, and confounded me with the sense of mine own ignorance; for there never came a thought into my heart before now that showed me so the beauty of Jesus Christ. It made me love a holy life, and long to do something for the honor and glory of the name of the Lord Jesus. Yea, I thought that had I now a thousand gallons of blood in my body, I could spill it all for the sake of the Lord Jesus.

# 36

# ARGUMENT WITH IGNORANCE, OF IGNORANCE

I SAW THEN in my dream, that Hopeful looked back, and saw Ignorance, whom they had left behind, coming after. Look, said he to Christian, how far yonder youngster loitereth behind.

CHRISTIAN: Aye, aye, I see him: he careth not for our company.

HOPEFUL: But I trow it would not have hurt him, had he kept pace with us hitherto.

CHRISTIAN: That is true; but I warrant you he thinketh otherwise.

HOPEFUL: That I think he doth; but, however, let us tarry for him. (So they did.)

Then Christian said to him, Come away, man; why do you stay so behind?

IGNORANCE: I take my pleasure in walking alone, even more a great deal than in company, unless I like it the better.

Then said Christian to Hopeful, (but softly,) Did I

not tell you he cared not for our company? But, however, said he, come up, and let us talk away the time in this solitary place. Then, directing his speech to Ignorance, he said, Come, how do you do? How stands it between God and your soul now?

IGNORANCE: I hope, well; for I am always full of good motions, that come into my mind to comfort me as I walk.

CHRISTIAN: What good motions? Pray tell us.

IGNORANCE: Why, I think of God and heaven.

CHRISTIAN: So do the devils and damned souls.

IGNORANCE: But I think of them, and desire them.

CHRISTIAN: So do many that are never like to come there. "The soul of the sluggard desireth, and hath nothing."

*Proverbs 13:4*

IGNORANCE: But I think of them, and leave all for them.

CHRISTIAN: That I doubt: for to leave all is a very hard matter; yea, a harder matter than many are aware of. But why, or by what, art thou persuaded that thou hast left all for God and heaven?

IGNORANCE: My heart tells me so.

CHRISTIAN: The wise man says, "He that trusteth in his own heart is a fool."

*Proverbs 28:26*

IGNORANCE: That is spoken of an evil heart; but mine is a good one.

CHRISTIAN: But how dost thou prove that?

IGNORANCE: It comforts me in hopes of heaven.

CHRISTIAN: That may be through its deceitfulness; for a man's heart may minister comfort to him in the hopes of that thing for which he has yet no ground to hope.

IGNORANCE: But my heart and life agree together; and therefore my hope is well-grounded.

CHRISTIAN: Who told thee that thy heart and life agree together?

IGNORANCE: My heart tells me so.

CHRISTIAN: "Ask my fellow if I be a thief." Thy heart tells thee so! Except the word of God beareth witness in this matter, other testimony is of no value.

IGNORANCE: But is it not a good heart that hath good thoughts? and is not that a good life that is according to God's commandments?

CHRISTIAN: Yes, that is a good heart that hath good thoughts, and that is a good life that is according to God's commandments; but it is one thing indeed to have these, and another thing only to think so.

IGNORANCE: Pray, what count you good thoughts, and a life according to God's commandments?

CHRISTIAN: There are good thoughts of divers kinds; some respecting ourselves, some God, some Christ, and some other things.

IGNORANCE: What be good thoughts respecting ourselves?

CHRISTIAN: Such as agree with the word of God.

IGNORANCE: When do our thoughts of ourselves agree with the word of God?

CHRISTIAN: When we pass the same judgment upon ourselves which the word passes. To explain myself: the word of God saith of persons in a natural condition, "There is none righteous, there is none that doeth good." It saith also, that, "every imagination of the heart of man is only evil, and that continually." And again, "The imagination of man's heart is evil from his youth." Now, then, when we think thus of ourselves, having sense thereof, then are our thoughts good ones, because according to the word of God.

*Genesis 6:5*
*Romans 3:10, 12*

*Genesis 8:21*

IGNORANCE: I will never believe that my heart is thus bad.

CHRISTIAN: Therefore thou never hadst one good thought concerning thyself in thy life. But let me go on. As the word passeth a judgment upon our hearts, so it passeth a judgment upon our ways; and when the thoughts of our hearts and ways agree with the judgment which the word giveth of both, then are both good, because agreeing thereto.

IGNORANCE: Make out your meaning.

CHRISTIAN: Why, the word of God saith, that man's ways are crooked ways, not good but perverse; it saith, they are naturally out of the good way, that they have not known it. Now, when a man thus thinketh of his ways, I say, when he doth sensibly, and with heart-humiliation, thus think, then hath he good thoughts of his own ways, because his thoughts now agree with the judgment of the word of God.

*Psalm 125:5*
*Proverbs 2:15*
*Romans 3:12*

IGNORANCE: What are good thoughts concerning God?

CHRISTIAN: Even, as I have said concerning ourselves, when our thoughts of God do agree with what the word saith of him; and that is, when we think of his being and attributes as the word hath taught, of which I cannot now discourse at large. But to speak of him with reference to us: then have we right thoughts of God when we think that he knows us better than we know ourselves, and can see sin in us when and where we can see none in ourselves; when we think he knows our inmost thoughts, and that our heart, with all its depths, is always open unto his eyes; also when we think that all our righteousness stinks in his nostrils, and that therefore he cannot abide to see us stand before him in any confidence, even in all our best performances.

IGNORANCE: Do you think that I am such a fool as to think that God can see no further than I; or that I would come to God in the best of my performances?

CHRISTIAN: Why, how dost thou think in this matter?

IGNORANCE: Why, to be short, I think I must believe in Christ for justification.

CHRISTIAN: How! think thou must believe in Christ, when thou seest not thy need of him! Thou neither seest thy original nor actual infirmities; but hast such an opinion of thyself, and of what thou doest, as plainly renders thee to be one that did never see the necessity of Christ's personal righteousness to justify thee before God. How, then, dost thou say, I believe in Christ?

IGNORANCE: I believe well enough, for all that.

CHRISTIAN: How dost thou believe?

IGNORANCE: I believe that Christ died for sinners; and that I shall be justified before God from the curse, through his gracious acceptance of my obedience to his laws. Or thus, Christ makes my duties, that are religious, acceptable to his Father by virtue of his merits, and so shall I be justified.

CHRISTIAN: Let me give an answer to this confession of thy faith.

Thou believest with a fantastical faith; for this faith is nowhere described in the word.

Thou believest with a false faith; because it taketh justification from the personal righteousness of Christ, and applies it to thy own.

This faith maketh not Christ a justifier of thy person, but of thy actions; and of thy person for thy action's sake, which is false.

Therefore this faith is deceitful, even such as will leave thee under wrath in the day of God Almighty: for true justifying faith puts the soul, as sensible of its lost condition by the law, upon flying for refuge unto Christ's righteousness; (which righteousness of his is not an act of grace by which he maketh, for justification, thy obedience accepted with God, but his personal obedience to the law, in doing and suffering for us what that required at our hands;) this righteousness, I say, true faith accepteth; under the skirt of which the soul being shrouded, and by it presented as spotless before God, it is accepted, and acquitted from condemnation.

IGNORANCE: What! would you have us trust to what Christ in his own person has done without us? This conceit would loosen the reins of our lust, and tolerate us to live as we list: for what matter how we live, if we may be justified by Christ's personal righteousness from all, when we believe it?

CHRISTIAN: Ignorance is thy name, and as thy name is, so art thou: even this thy answer demonstrateth what I say. Ignorant thou art of what justifying righteousness is, and as ignorant how to secure thy soul, through the faith of it, from the heavy wrath of God. Yea, thou also art ignorant of the true effects of saving faith in this righteousness of Christ, which is to bow and win over the heart to God in Christ, to love his name, his word, ways, and people, and not as thou ignorantly imaginest.

HOPEFUL: Ask him if ever he had Christ revealed to him from heaven.

IGNORANCE: What! you are a man for revelations! I do believe, that what both you and all the rest of you say about that matter, is but the fruit of distracted brains.

HOPEFUL: Why, man, Christ is so hid in God from the natural apprehensions of the flesh, that he cannot by any man be savingly known, unless God the Father reveals him to him.

IGNORANCE: That is your faith, but not mine, yet mine, I doubt not, is as good as yours, though I have not in my head so many whimsies as you.

CHRISTIAN: Give me leave to put in a word. You ought not so slightly to speak of this matter: for this I will boldly affirm, even as my good companion hath done, that no man can know Jesus

Christ but by the revelation of the Father: yea, and faith too, by which the soul layeth hold upon Christ, (if it be right,) must be wrought by the exceeding greatness of his mighty power, the working of which faith, I perceive, poor Ignorance, thou art ignorant of. Be awakened, then, see thine own wretchedness, and fly to the Lord Jesus; and by his righteousness, which is the righteousness of God, (for he himself is God,) thou shalt be delivered from condemnation.

*Matthew 11:27*
*1 Corinthians 12:3*
*Ephesians 1:17–19*

IGNORANCE: You go so fast I cannot keep pace with you; do you go on before: I must stay a while behind.

Then they said,

"Well, Ignorance, wilt thou yet foolish be,
To slight good counsel, ten times given thee?
And if thou yet refuse it, thou shalt know,
Ere long, the evil of thy doing so.
Remember, man, in time: stoop, do not fear:
Good counsel, taken well, saves; therefore hear.
But if thou yet shalt slight it, thou wilt be
The loser, Ignorance, I'll warrant thee."

Then Christian addressed himself thus to his fellow:

CHRISTIAN: Well, come, my good Hopeful, I perceive that thou and I must walk by ourselves again.

So I saw in my dream, that they went on apace before, and Ignorance he came hobbling after. Then said Christian to his companion, I much pity this poor man: it will certainly go ill with him at last.

HOPEFUL: Alas! there are abundance in our town in his condition, whole families, yea, whole streets, and that of pilgrims too; and if there be so many in our parts, how many, think you, must there be in the place where he was born?

CHRISTIAN: Indeed, the word saith, "He hath blinded their eyes, lest they should see," etc.

But, now we are by ourselves, what do you think of such men? Have they at no time, think you, convictions of sin, and so, consequently, fears that their state is dangerous?

HOPEFUL: Nay, do you answer that question yourself, for you are the elder man.

CHRISTIAN: Then I say, sometimes (as I think) they may; but they being naturally ignorant, understand not that such convictions tend to their good; and therefore they do desperately seek to stifle them, and presumptuously continue to flatter themselves in the way of their own hearts.

HOPEFUL: I do believe, as you say, that fear tends much to men's good, and to make them right at their beginning to go on pilgrimage.

*Job 28:28*
*Psalm 111:10*
*Proverbs 1:7; 9:10*

CHRISTIAN: Without all doubt it doth, if it be right; for so says the word, "The fear of the Lord is the beginning of wisdom."

HOPEFUL: How will you describe right fear?

CHRISTIAN: True or right fear is discovered by three things:

1. By its rise; it is caused by saving convictions for sin.

2. It driveth the soul to lay fast hold of Christ for salvation.

3. It begetteth and continueth in the soul a great reverence of God, his word, and ways; keeping it tender, and making it afraid to turn from them, to the right hand or to the left, to any thing that may dishonor God, break its peace, grieve the Spirit, or cause the enemy to speak reproachfully.

HOPEFUL: Well said; I believe you have said the truth. Are we now almost got past the Enchanted Ground?

CHRISTIAN: Why? are you weary of this discourse?

HOPEFUL: No, verily, but that I would know where we are.

CHRISTIAN: We have not now above two miles further to go thereon. But let us return to our matter.

Now, the ignorant know not that such conviction as tend to put them in fear, are for their good, and therefore they seek to stifle them.

HOPEFUL: How do they seek to stifle them?

CHRISTIAN: 1. They think that those fears are wrought by the devil, (though indeed they are wrought of God,) and thinking so, they resist them, as things that directly tend to their overthrow.

2. They also think that these fears tend to the spoiling of their faith; when, alas for them, poor men that they are, they have none at all; and therefore they harden their hearts against them.

3. They presume they ought not to fear, and therefore, in despite of them, wax presumptuously confident.

4. They see that those fears tend to take away from them their pitiful old self-holiness, and therefore they resist them with all their might.

HOPEFUL: I know something of this myself; for before I knew myself it was so with me.

CHRISTIAN: Well, we will leave, at this time, our neighbor Ignorance by himself, and fall upon another profitable question.

HOPEFUL: With all my heart; but you shall still begin.

# 37

# Temporary,
# Beulah Land

CHRISTIAN: Well then, did you not know, about ten years ago, one Temporary in your parts, who was a forward man in religion then?

HOPEFUL: Know him! yes; he dwelt in Graceless, a town about two miles off of Honesty, and he dwelt next door to one Turnback.

CHRISTIAN: Right; he dwelt under the same roof with him. Well, that man was much awakened once: I believe that then he had some sight of his sins, and of the wages that were due thereto.

HOPEFUL: I am of your mind, for (my house not being above three miles from him) he would oft-times come to me, and that with many tears. Truly I pitied the man, and was not altogether without hope of him; but one may see, it is not every one that cries, "Lord, Lord!"

CHRISTIAN: He told me once that he was resolved to go on pilgrimage, as we go now; but all of a sudden he grew acquainted with one Save-self, and then he became a stranger to me.

HOPEFUL: Now, since we are talking about him, let us a little inquire into the reason of the

sudden backsliding of him and such others.

CHRISTIAN: It may be very profitable; but do you begin.

HOPEFUL: Well, then, there are, in my judgment, four reasons for it:

1. Though the consciences of such men are awakened, yet their minds are not changed:

therefore, when the power of guilt weareth away, that which provoked them to be religious ceaseth; wherefore they naturally turn to their own course again; even as we see the dog that is sick of what he hath eaten, so long as his sickness prevails, he vomits and casts up all; not that he doth this of a free mind, (if we may say a dog has a mind,) but because it troubleth his stomach: but now, when his sickness is over, and so his stomach eased, his desires being not at all alienated from his vomit, he turns him about, and licks up all; and so it is true which is written, "The dog is turned to his own vomit again." Thus, I say, being hot for heaven, by virtue only of the sense and fear of the torments of hell, as their sense and fear of damnation chills and cools, so their desires for heaven and salvation cool also. So then it comes to pass, that when their guilt and fear is gone, their desires for heaven and happiness die, and they return to their course again.

*2 Peter 2:22*

2. Another reason is, they have slavish fears that do overmaster them: I speak now of the fears that they have of men; "For the fear of man bringeth a snare." So then, though they seem to be hot for heaven so long as the flames of hell are about their ears, yet, when that terror is a little over, they betake themselves to second thoughts, namely, that it is good to be wise and not to run (for they know not what) the hazard of losing all, or at least of bringing themselves into unavoidable and unnecessary troubles; and so they fall in with the world again.

*Proverbs 29:25*

3. The shame that attends religion lies also as a block in their way: they are proud and haughty, and religion in their eye is low and contemptible: therefore when they have lost their sense of hell and the wrath to come, they return again to their former course.

4. Guilt, and to meditate terror, are grievous to them; they like not to see their misery before they come into it; though perhaps the sight of at it first, if they loved that sight, might make them fly whither the righteous fly and are safe; but because they do, as I hinted before, even shun the thoughts of guilt and terror, therefore, when once they are rid of their awakenings about the terrors and wrath of God, they harden their hearts gladly, and choose such ways as will harden them more and more.

CHRISTIAN: You are pretty near the business, for the bottom of all is for want of a change in their mind and will. And therefore they are but like the felon that standeth before the judge: he quakes and trembles, and seems to repent most heartily, but the bottom of all is the fear of the halter: not that he hath any detestation of the offence, as it is evident; because, let but this man have his liberty, and he will be a thief, and so a rogue still; whereas, if his mind was changed, he would be otherwise.

HOPEFUL: Now I have showed you the reason of their going back, do you show me the manner thereof.

CHRISTIAN: So I will willingly.

1. They draw off their thoughts, all that they may, from the remembrance of God, death, and judgment to come.

2. Then they cast off by degrees private duties, as closet prayer, curbing their lusts, watching, sorrow for sin, and the like.

3. Then they shun the company of lively and warm Christians.

4. After that, they grow cold to public duty, as hearing, reading, godly conference, and the like.

5. They then begin to pick holes, as we say, in the coats of some of the godly, and that devilishly, that they may have a seeming color to throw religion (for the sake of some infirmities they have espied in them) behind their backs.

6. Then they begin to adhere to, and associate themselves with, carnal, loose, and wanton men.

7. Then they give way to carnal and wanton discourses in secret; and glad are they if they can see such things in any that are counted honest, that they may the more boldly do it through their example.

8. After this they begin to play with little sins openly.

9. And then, being hardened, they show themselves as they are. Thus, being launched again into the gulf of misery, unless a miracle of grace prevent it, they everlastingly perish in their own deceivings.

Isaiah 62:4–12
Song 2:10–12

Now I saw in my dream, that by this time the pilgrims were got over the Enchanted Ground, and entering into the country of Beulah, whose air was very sweet and pleasant, the way lying directly through it, they solaced themselves there for a season. Yea, here they heard continually the singing of birds, and saw every day the flowers appear in the earth, and heard the voice of the turtle in the land. In this country the sun shineth night and day: wherefore this was beyond the Valley of the Shadow of Death, and also out of the reach of Giant Despair; neither could they from this place so much as see Doubting Castle. Here they were within sight of the city they were going to; also here met them some of the inhabitants thereof; for in this land the shining ones commonly walked, because it was upon the borders of heaven. In this land also the contract between the Bride and the Bridegroom was renewed; yea, here, "as the bridegroom rejoiceth over the bride, so doth God rejoice over them." Here they had no want of corn and wine; for in this place they met with abundance of what they had sought for in all their pilgrimage. Here they heard voices from out of the city, loud voices, saying, "Say ye to the daughter of Zion, Behold, thy salvation cometh! Behold, his reward is with him!" Here all the inhabitants of the country called them "the holy People, the redeemed of the Lord, sought out," etc.

Now, as they walked in this land, they had more rejoicing than in parts more remote from the kingdom to which they were bound; and drawing near to the city, they had yet a more perfect view thereof: It was builded of pearls and precious stones, also the streets thereof were paved with gold; so that, by reason of the natural glory of the city, and the reflection of the sunbeams upon it, Christian with desire fell sick; Hopeful also had a fit or two of the same disease: wherefore here they lay by it a while, crying out because of their pangs, "If you see my

Beloved, tell him that I am sick of love."

But, being a little strengthened, and better able to bear their sickness, they walked on their way, and came yet nearer and nearer, where were orchards, vineyards, and gardens, and their gates opened into the highway. Now, as they came up to these places, behold the gardener stood in the way; to whom the pilgrims said, Whose goodly vineyards and gardens are these? He answered, they are the King's, and are planted here for his own delight, and also for the solace of pilgrims. So the gardener had them into the vineyards, and bid them refresh themselves with the dainties ; he also showed them there the King's walks and arbors where he delighted to be: And here they tarried and slept. *Deuteronomy 23:24*

Now I beheld in my dream, that they talked more in their sleep at this time than ever they did in all their journey; and, being in a muse thereabout, the gardener said even to me, Wherefore musest thou at the matter? It is the nature of the fruit of the grapes of these vineyards, "to go down so sweetly as to cause the lips of them that are asleep to speak." *Song 7:9*

So I saw that when they awoke, they addressed themselves to go up to the city. But, as I said, the reflection of the sun upon the city (for the city was pure gold *Revelation 21:18* ) was so extremely glorious, that they could not as yet with open face behold it, but through an instrument made for that purpose. So I saw, that as they went on, *2 Corinthians 3:18* there met them two men in raiment that shone like gold, also their faces shone as the light.

These men asked the pilgrims whence they came; and they told them. They also asked them where they had lodged, what difficulties and dangers, what comforts and pleasures, they had met with in the way; and they told them. Then said the men that met them, You have but two difficulties more to meet with, and then you are in the City.

Christian then and his companion asked the men to go along with them: so they told them that they would; But, said they, you must obtain it by your own faith. So I saw in my dream, that they went on together till they came in sight of the gate.

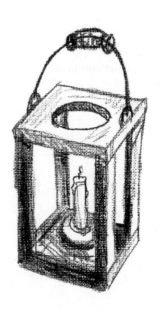

# 38

# River of Death,
# Shining Ones

NOW I further saw, that betwixt them and the gate was a river; but there was no bridge to go over, and the river was very deep. At the sight, therefore, of this river the pilgrims were much stunned; but the men that went with them said, You must go through, or you cannot come at the gate.

The pilgrims then began to inquire if there was no other way to the gate. To which they answered, Yes; but there hath not any, save two, to wit, Enoch and Elijah, been permitted to tread that path since the foundation of the world, nor shall until the last trumpet shall sound. The pilgrims then, especially Christian, began to despond in their mind, and looked this way and that, but no way could be found by them by which they might escape the river. Then they asked the men if the waters were all of a depth. They said, No; yet they could not help them in that case; for, said they, you shall find it deeper or shallower as you believe in the King of the place.

Then they addressed themselves to the water, and entering, Christian began to sink, and crying out to his good friend Hopeful, he said, I sink in deep waters; the billows go over my head; all his waves go over me. Selah.

Then said the other, Be of good cheer, my brother:

I feel the bottom, and it is good. Then said Christian, Ah! my friend, the sorrows of death have compassed me about, I shall not see the land that flows with milk and honey. And with that a great darkness and horror fell upon Christian, so that he could not see before him. Also here he in a great measure lost his senses, so that he could neither remember nor orderly talk of any of those sweet refreshments that he had met with in the way of his pilgrimage. But all the words that he spoke still tended to discover that he had horror of mind, and heart-fears that he should die in that river, and never obtain entrance in at the gate. Here also, as they that stood by perceived, he was much in the troublesome thoughts of the sins that he had committed, both since and before he began to be a pilgrim. It was also observed that he was troubled with apparitions of hobgoblins and evil spirits; for ever and anon he would intimate so much by words.

Hopeful therefore here had much ado to keep his brother's head above water; yea, sometimes he would be quite gone down, and then, ere a while, he would rise up again half dead. Hopeful did also endeavor to comfort him, saying, Brother, I see the gate, and men standing by to receive us; but Christian would answer, It is you, it is you they wait for; for you have been hopeful ever since I knew you. And so have you, said he to Christian. Ah, brother, (said he,) surely if I was right he would now arise to help me; but for my sins he hath brought me into the snare, and hath left me. Then said Hopeful, My brother, you have quite forgot the text where it is said of the wicked, "There are no bands in their death, but their strength is firm; they are not troubled as other men, neither are they plagued like other men." These troubles and distresses that you go through in these waters, are no sign that God hath forsaken you; but are sent to try you, whether you will call to mind that which heretofore you have received of his goodness, and live upon him in your distresses.

*Psalm 73:4–5*

Then I saw in my dream, that Christian was in a muse a while. To whom also Hopeful added these words, Be of good cheer, Jesus Christ maketh thee whole. And with that Christian brake out with a loud voice, Oh, I see him again; and he tells me, "When thou passest through the waters, I will be with thee; and through the rivers, they shall not overflow thee." Then they both took courage, and the enemy was after that as still as a

*Isaiah 43:2*

stone, until they were gone over. Christian, therefore, presently found ground to stand upon, and so it followed that the rest of the river was but shallow. Thus they got over.

Now, upon the bank of the river, on the other side, they saw the two shining men again, who there waited for them. Wherefore, being come out of the river, they saluted them, saying, We are ministering spirits, sent forth to minister for those that shall be the heirs of salvation. Thus they went along towards the gate.

Now you must note, that the city stood upon a mighty hill; but the pilgrims went up that hill with ease, because they had these two men to lead them up by the arms: they had likewise left their mortal garments behind them in the river; for though they went in with them, they came out without them. They therefore went up here with much agility and speed, though the foundation upon which the city was framed was higher than the clouds; they therefore went up through the region of the air, sweetly talking as they went, being comforted because they safely got over the river, and had such glorious companions to attend them.

The talk that they had with the shining ones was about the glory of the place; who told them that the beauty and glory of it was inexpressible. There, said they, is "Mount Sion, the heavenly Jerusalem, the innumerable company of angels, and the spirits of just men made *Hebrews 12:22–24* perfect." You are going now, said they, to the paradise of God, wherein you shall see the tree of life, and eat of the never-fading fruits thereof: and when you come there you shall have white robes given you, and your walk and talk shall be every day with the King, even all the days *Revelation 2:7; 3:4–5; 22:5* of eternity. There you shall not see again such things as you saw when you were in the lower region upon earth; to wit, sorrow, sickness, affliction, and death; "For the *Revelation 2 1:4* former things are passed away." You are going now to

Abraham, to Isaac, and Jacob, and to the prophets, men that God hath taken away from the evil to come, and that are now "resting upon their beds, each one walking in his righteousness." The men then asked, What must we do in the holy place? To whom it was answered, You must there receive the comfort of all your toil, and have joy for all your sorrow; you must reap what you have sown, even the fruit of all your prayers, and tears, and sufferings for the King by the way. In that place you *Galatians 6:7–8* must wear crowns of gold, and enjoy the perpetual sight and vision of the Holy One; for "there you shall see him as he is." There also you shall serve him continually *1 John 3:2* with praise, with shouting and thanksgiving, whom you desired to serve in the world, though with much difficulty, because of the infirmity of your flesh. There your eyes shall be delighted with seeing, and your ears with hearing the pleasant voice of the Mighty One. There you shall enjoy your friends again that are gone thither before you; and there you shall with joy receive even every one that follows into the holy place after you. There also you shall be clothed with glory and majesty, and put into an equipage fit to ride out with the King of Glory. When he shall come with sound of trumpet in the clouds, as upon the wings of the wind, you shall come with him; and when he shall sit upon the throne of judgment, you shall sit by him; yea, and when he shall pass sentence upon all the workers of iniquity, let them be angels or men, you also shall have a voice in that *1 Thessalonians 4:14–17* judgment, because they were his and your enemies. Also, *Jude 14–15* when he shall again return to the city, you shall go too *Daniel 7:9–10* with sound of trumpet, and be ever with him. *1 Corinthians 6:2–3*

# 39

# CELESTIAL CITY,
## CONCLUSION

N OW, WHILE they were thus drawing towards the gate, behold a company of the heavenly host came out to meet them: to whom it was said by the other two shining ones, These are the men that have loved our Lord when they were in the world, and that have left all for his holy name; and he hath sent us to fetch them, and we have brought them thus far on their desired journey, that they may go in and look their Redeemer in the face with joy. Then the heavenly host gave a great shout, saying, "Blessed are they that are called to the marriage-supper of the Lamb." There came out also at this time to meet them several of the King's trumpeters, clothed in white and shining raiment, who, with melodious noises and loud, made even the heavens to echo with their sound. These trumpeters saluted Christian and his fellow with ten thousand welcomes from the world; and this they did with shouting and sound of trumpet.

*Revelation 19:9*

This done, they compassed them round on every side; some went before, some behind, and some on the right hand, and some on the left, (as it were to guard them through the upper regions,) continually sounding as they went, with melodious noise, in notes on high; so that the very sight was to them that could behold it as if heaven itself was come down to meet them. Thus, therefore, they walked on together; and, as they walked,

ever and anon these trumpeters, even with joyful sound, would, by mixing their music with looks and gestures, still signify to Christian and his brother how welcome they were into their company, and with what gladness they came to meet them. And now were these two men, as it were, in heaven, before they came to it, being swallowed up with the sight of angels, and with hearing of their melodious notes. Here also they had the city itself in view; and they thought they heard all the bells therein to ring, to welcome them thereto. But, above all, the warm and joyful thoughts that they had about their own dwelling there with such company, and that for ever and ever; oh, by what tongue or pen can their glorious joy be expressed! Thus they came up to the gate.

Now when they were come up to the gate, there was written over it, in letters of gold, "blessed are they that do his commandments, that they may have right to the tree of life, and may enter in through the gates into the city."

Then I saw in my dream, that the shining men bid them call at the gate: the which when they did, some from above looked over the gate, to wit, Enoch, Moses, and Elijah, etc., to whom it was said, These pilgrims are come from the City of Destruction, for the love that they bear to the King of this place; and then the pilgrims gave in unto them each man his certificate, which they had received in the beginning: those therefore were carried in unto the King, who, when he had read them, said, Where are the men? To whom it was answered, They are standing without the gate. The King then commanded to open the gate, "That the righteous nation (said he) that keepeth the truth may enter in." _Isaiah 26:2_

Now I saw in my dream, that these two men went in at the gate; and lo, as they entered, they were transfigured; and they had raiment put on that shone like gold. There were also that met them with harps and crowns, and gave them to them; the harps to praise withal, and the crowns in token of honor. Then I heard in my dream, that all the bells in the city rang again for joy, and that it was said unto them,

"enter ye into the joy of your lord."

I also heard the men themselves, that they sang with a loud voice, saying,

"blessing, and honor, and glory, and power, be unto him that sitteth upon the throne, and unto the lamb, for ever and ever."

Now, just as the gates were opened to let in the men, I looked in after them, and behold the city shone like the sun; the streets also were paved with gold; and in them walked many men, with crowns on their heads, palms in their hands, and golden harps, to sing praises withal.

There were also of them that had wings, and they answered one another without intermission, saying, Holy, holy, holy is the Lord. And after that they shut up the gates; which, when I had seen, I wished myself among them.

Now, while I was gazing upon all these things, I turned my head to look back, and saw Ignorance come up to the river side; but he soon got over, and that without half the difficulty which the other two men met with. For it happened that there was then in that place one Vain-Hope, a ferryman, that with his boat helped him over; so he, as the other I saw, did ascend the hill, to come up to the gate; only he came alone, neither did any man meet him with the least encouragement. When he was come up to the gate, he looked up to the writing that was above, and then began to knock, supposing that entrance should have been quickly administered to him; but he was asked by the men that looked over the top of the gate, Whence come you? and what would you have? He answered, I have ate and drank in the presence of the King, and he has taught in our streets. Then they asked him for his certificate, that they might go in and show it to the King: so he fumbled in his bosom for one, and found none. Then said they, Have you none? but the man answered never a word. So they told the King, but he would not come down to see him, but command-ed the two shining ones, that conducted Christian and Hopeful to the city, to go out and take Ignorance, and bind him hand and foot, and have him away. Then they took him up, and carried him through the air to the door that I saw in the side of the hill, and put him in there. Then I saw that there was a way to hell, even from the gate of heaven, as well as from the City of Destruction. So I awoke, and behold it was a dream.

Now, reader, I have told my dream to thee,
See if thou canst interpret it to me,
Or to thyself, or neighbor: but take heed
Of misinterpreting; for that, instead
Of doing good, will but thyself abuse:
By misinterpreting, evil ensues.
Take heed, also, that thou be not extreme
In playing with the outside of my dream;
Nor let my figure or similitude
Put thee into a laughter, or a feud.
Leave this for boys and fools; but as for thee,
Do thou the substance of my matter see.
Put by the curtains, look within my veil,
Turn up my metaphors, and do not fail.
There, if thou seekest them, such things thou'lt find
As will be helpful to an honest mind.
What of my dross thou findest there, be bold
To throw away, but yet preserve the gold.
What if my gold be wrapped up in ore?
None throw away the apple for the core:
But if thou shalt cast all away as vain,
I know not but 't will make me dream again.

# INDEX